SUMMARY

I0008401

ACKNOWLEDGMENTS

First I would like to thank God as the great spirit capable of giving me the strength and motivation necessary to complete this project .

I am fully grateful to my special girl, Katiucia Capiotti, for all the encouragement, love, trust, support and patience during this endeavor. Without this care, certainly, my way would have been much more difficult.

Thanks to my mother, Lilian, my father Nelson and my sister Bruna, for all the good words and unconditional family love.

I would like to express all my gratitude to my advisor, Profª. Drª. Mara Abel, who captivated me from the start with her competence and professionalism. Surely, you are a great inspiration for everyone who work with you. Thanks to Rafael Port da Rocha, my co-advisor, for his competence, dynamism and his innovative visions. Thanks to the fellow Victor Rey and to my colleagues from the Intelligent Databases Group, Sandro Fiorini, Joel Carbonera and Alexandre Lorenzatti for the dedication during the construction of this work. Thank you for all the transmitted knowledge and for all the good philosophical conversations. I also thank the staff of the geology area, Ariane Bernardes and Eduardo Espindola for their dedication during this project .

I especially thank my partner Tagline Treichel and our entire company staff, for all patience, tolerance and encouragement given to me.

Finally, I thank all my good friends, who are really important in my life. Thank you all.

INTRODUCTION

Ontology (Greek oints and logoi, "knowledge of being") is the part of philosophy that deals with the nature of being, reality, the existence of beings and metaphysical issues in general (Wikipedia 2012). Although it is a modern term, their study began with Aristotle, the Greek philosopher who explored meticulously the division of being into existence and essence. Ontologies are intended to explain and formalize the existence of a systematic way, dealing with kinds and structures of objects, properties, events, processes and relations belonging to a certain portion of reality, in a given domain of interest. Thus, act as infrastructure in facilitating and creating a common understanding and shared [36].

Since ancient times, the description and sharing of the meaning of the things of the world have been giving support to communication within a community and developed a sophisticated survival mechanism for the species. Communication allows the transfer of experience between humans and the collective construction of solutions, increasing the environment control capacity.

Ontologies can be used in various ways as intelligent integration of information, natural language processing, knowledge management, e-commerce, etc. [10]. Moreover, they have been recognized as an essential layer in the Semantic Web emerging [4]. The global information is growing at great speed, hence the need to reuse of ontologies is crucial to assist the development and maintenance of efficient systems and solutions based on knowledge.

As ontologies are used in many different purposes, Jasper (1999) proposed a new definition for the word ontology for this concept to be more widespread in other communities than only in knowledge engineering, software engineering or database communities. The definition given by Jasper was that "An ontology may take many forms, but necessarily includes a vocabulary of terms and some specification of their meaning. This includes definitions and an indication of how concepts are inter-related, which collectively imposes a structure on the domain and restricts the possibility of terms interpretation." Actually, there are several ontological definitions, some more independent and others more dependent on the development process. However, each proposed definition seeks complementary views of the same reality. In fact, the ultimate goal of conceptualizing and correctly defining the term ontology is to establish consensual knowledge in a generic way [6].

According to Studer [33], a highly informal ontology is not an ontology because it can not be understood by a computer. For this reason, an ontology must be represented by a formal language, allowing the use of automated foundational (inference) and communication. Representation by a language also allows the ontology to be shared among users, especially the Web, since the members of a community that shares knowledge usually are physically separated.

There are several formal languages available, each one with benefits and limitations. However, some more modern ones are suggested and recommended by the World Wide Web Consortium (W3C) and form the basis of the Semantic Web. Resource Description Framework (RDF) is a language for modeling metadata representing descriptions of conceptual resources. Web Ontology Language (OWL) is a language for knowledge representation which is based on RDF (can be seen as a metadata layer higher level on RDF) and is characterized by allowing the expression of formal semantics. According to the purpose of use, you can use one of the specializations available language OWL Lite, OWL DL, OWL Full.

In the process of knowledge engineering, the concern usually revolves around the collection of shared knowledge within a particular community and the storage of this knowledge as a formal ontology that can be reused for various purposes. Therefore, an ontology is defined as a formal specification of a shared conceptualization [5]. The knowledge can be enriched if the communities communicate with each other, overcoming the barriers of different representations and focusing on converting the shared conceptualization into valid and efficient domain ontologies. If the sharing and reuse of ontologies increases their quality [20], it is necessary to share the meaning of terms in a given domain (Jasper et al. 1999).

However, even in the same domain, the sharing and construction of ontology vocabularies can bring unexpected difficulties. Users can give different names for the same concept (synonymy) or may use the same word to refer to different concepts (false match). In addition, information domains are not fixed or static: they evolve when missing elements become part of the domain or when some elements become [30] As common knowledge is constantly evolving, these changes need to be adapted to the domain model, updating the ontology by adding or removing concepts or relationships. Thus, collaboration has become an important part of the process of ontology development, assisting with the explanation of the concept behind the vocabulary and with the evolution of the vocabulary to its new meanings.

With this point of view, we know that the extraction of knowledge and its formalization in an ontology is an arduous process. The difficulty of classifying the entities of the world is a conceptual problem, where each individual has its own abstraction of reality. This difficulty is further aggravated when several people discuss the same shared conceptual model, when divergent ideas and conceptualizations can arise. Based on this difficulty, various collaboration tools for ontology construction have emerged in the past years. These approaches seek to provide a shared template and record the changes made by the experts, seeking to reduce the time required to build an ontology efficient. However, current solutions do not provide sufficient constructs for a complete semantic capture of the process of conceptualizing and the concepts themselves, or lack sufficient accuracy. Thus, the discussion of meaning becomes a hard task because there are not enough constructs to explicit desired representations. Moreover, some tools are directly related to representation languages such as OWL, which are difficult to use by users who do not know the language deeply.

Consensus building and collaborative problem solving is a process that allows members of a team with common interests to work together to develop a solution acceptable by all. When everyone agree and are satisfied with the final proposal we say that consensus was reached. All members shall have equal voting rights, veto and opinion, and should be involved in the process cooperatively.

Collaboration also improves the quality of the produced models since they incorporate different perspectives of the team members.

According to Guizzardi [17], the conversational maximum for building conceptual models is that the message should be relevant full, clear, unambiguous, brief, without excess of information and true according to the point of view of the sender' knowledge. However, to capture the correct meaning of a concept, it is necessary to allow the individual to express their understanding of this concept through the use of properties that have specific meaning for him. This is the role of Foundational Ontologies: express the inherent properties that provide identity to objects in some world. This study aims to provide support to the foundational concepts to achieve more accuracy in the formalization of meaning.

Furthermore, we understand that the human being has the vision as the first and most important way to capture information from the external world and generate their conceptualizations. This is even more true in imagistic domains such as Sedimentology, where we develop our study, in which the visual pattern recognition is the initial process to capture information and support to problem solving. Thus, this work helps on providing specialists with the support needed to build conceptual models of visual knowledge, taking advantage of the visual representation and images to help express the full meaning of the concepts.

In our approach, the collaborative construction of ontologies is based on information about the concepts which is represented by metadata. These metadata provide the basis by which users can express their understanding of the meaning of concepts using a specific vocabulary, providing an ontological foundation to the homogeneous model. The use of metadata to describe ontological constructs and domain independent visual representations allows us to create an environment for the creation and evolution of domain ontologies without requiring users to have any prior knowledge about formal languages representation (which occurs with some current collaborative solutions), but providing mechanisms to manipulate visual information and to express symbolic and rich semantic models.

The ontologies developed assists the representation of concepts in visual domains through the collaborative construction of meaning supported by our proposed tool. The foundational ontology provides guidance to the anchoring of symbolic terms unambiguously, allowing users to negotiate the best representation of that meaning through discussions among themselves, also registered in the tool. It is

expected that this form of collective construction generates better models anchored in the reality to be captured.

The main contribution of this work is a metadata based approach to specify the ontological constructs and collaboration ontology independently of formal languages representation, through a collaborative environment for the construction and evolution of ontologies with an intuitive user interface.

The objectives of this work were:

a) provide a web-based system, accessible via web browser, which enables experts to directly change the ontology, recording the changes automatically.

b) provide ontological constructs of foundational to support the choices through the ontological expressiveness of a semantic foundational ontology;

c) provide visual ontological constructs to represent visual knowledge and support imagistic domains;

d) provide collaboration constructs for mapping the ontological changes and discussions held between community members.

We aim to generate, at the end of a process of collaboration, a robust domain ontology with greater precision in the specification of the concepts meaning and greater potential for integration with other applications. The capabilities of the metadata model and collaboration application proposed were evaluated through the collaborative construction of an ontology for describing sedimentary facies in the field of stratigraphy in Sedimentary Geology.

This work is structured as follows. In Chapter 2 we introduce basic concepts which are necessary for understanding the solutions presented in this work by addressing issues related to conceptual modeling, ontological foundation and visual knowledge. In Chapter 3 we present some of the main existing methodologies for ontology engineering and construction, as well as basic concepts for the collaborative development of ontologies. In addition, we present a comparative evaluation of the main collaborative tools that represent the state of the art in this area. In Chapter 4 we present the architec-

11

ture of the knowledge model based on metadata, which underlies the collaborative environment through metaontologies formalizing the representation of ontological constructs and the structure of the collaboration. In Chapter 5 we describe in detail the implementation of the collaborative application. Finally, in Chapter 7 we present the conclusions and anticipate some future work.

1 CONCEPTUAL MODELING

The conceptual modeling is responsible for identifying, analyzing and describing the concepts of a domain, as well as their semantic relationships, with the help of a modeling language based on a set of metaconcepts (forming a metamodel). The ontological modeling seeks to identify the concepts of a domain and specify them through an ontology with a specification language based on ontological categories independent domain (also called upper-level ontologies) [18].

An ontology aims on capturing the consensual knowledge that is accepted by a group [10]. In a practical view, an ontology is an explicit specification of a conceptualization. A conceptualization is an abstract, simplified view of the world is to be displayed. It is important that the group members are aligned with the same ontological commitment, meaning that they agree to use a shared vocabulary of terms in a coherent and consistent way [11]. Guarino expands the definition of Gruber establishing a paralalel with the use by Artificial Intelligence community, introducing that an ontology is an engineering artifact, constituted of a specific vocabulary used to describe a certain reality, along with explicit assumptions related to the intended meaning of the vocabulary words.

According to Guarino, an ontology is a logical theory that takes into account the intended meaning of a formal vocabulary, ie, the ontological commitment with a particular conceptualization of the world. Intentional models of a logical language using such a vocabulary are constrained by its ontological commitment. An ontology indirectly reflects this commitment (and the underlying conceptualization) by approaching these intentional models [13].

According to Guarino [13] both philosophy and computational definitions of ontology are related but have terminological differentiation. The philosophical definition defines the conceptualization while the computer definition defines ontology as an object of knowledge engineering. Thus, ontologies with different vocabularies can still share the same conceptualization.

Guarino defines the conceptual relations in a space domain (domain space), emphasizing that the focus is on the representation of the meaning of conceptual relations, also called intentional relations. Thus, the conceptual space can be defined as:

$$< D, W >$$

Where D is a domain of information and W is the set of all possible worlds (set of possible states that the domain can assume.) The conceptualization is the set of conceptual relations defined on a space domain, and can be represented as below, where R is the set of conceptual relations to space domain <D, W>.

$$C = < D, W, R >$$

The purpose of knowledge modeling is to elaborate models that correctly represent the domain. Thus, ontologically grounding the model avoids diversion and helps to create consistent ontologies. The ontological choices should be clear and explicit to allow mutual understanding, so it is necessary to explicit the intentional relationships and the meaning of the primitives of the representation language to be used to specify the knowledge. Guarino [14] established levels to classificate formalisms according to the types of primitives with which they are based on. The Table 1.1 shows the classification of the formalisms in detail.

Table 1.1 Classification of knowledge representation formalisms according to the use of primitives [14]

Level	Primitives	Interpretation	Main feature
Logical	Predicates and functions	Arbitrary	Formalization
Epistemological	Structural relations	Arbitrary	Structure
Ontological	Ontological relations	Restricted	Meaning
Conceptual	Conceptual relationships	Subjective	Conceptualization
Linguistic	Linguistic terms	Subjective	Dependence language

At the logical level, the primitives are the basic predicates and functions, which give formal semantics in terms of relations between domain objects. The relationships are generic and content independent. This formalizes the primitive level, but the interpretation of them is totally arbitrary.

At the epistemological level, we try to decrease the space between the logical level, where the primitives are extremely generic and the conceptual level, where meaning is given to the primitive. Thus, while the logical level deals with abstract predicates and the conceptual level with specific concepts, the declared primitives in the epistemological level allow a concept to be seen as a primitive for structuring knowledge. The structure of a concept in the epistemological level (corresponding to the unary predicate logic level) is described in terms of other concepts or binary relations (roles).

At the ontological level, the ontological commitments associated with the language primitives are explicitly specified by the semantic restriction of primitives or by meaning postulates introduced directly into the language. The goal is to restrict the possibility of differing interpretations. Thus, the ontological level focuses on establishing the significance of the domain in terms of primitives. You could say that a language is ontologically adequate if, at the syntactic level, she has enough granularity and the reification ability to express the meaning postulates of its own primitives, or if it is possible to give formal ontological interpretation to its primitives at the semantic level.

At the conceptual level, the primitives have well defined cognitive interpretations, corresponding to language-independent concepts.

The skeleton of the domain structure is defined and the knowledge is specified as a specialization of this skeleton. Definitions at this level may come together with definitions at the ontological level.

At the language level, primitives have to directly refer to terms such as verbs and nouns.

These definitions are important because the level of abstraction of knowledge must be defined before the modeling stage. A Knowledge can be specified at the conceptual level and never be implemented in a formal representation language. However, for purposes of communication and collaboration, the most interesting models in the context of this work are those that can be formalized in a language.

1.1 Ontological Metaproperties

In 1990 a methodology called OntoClean was proposed by Guarino [12], focused on the analysis of the meaning of concepts and properties of a domain in terms of how they relate in reality. This methodology guides the construction of knowledge models, providing a basis to represent ontological concepts in order to avoid misinterpretations and optimize the process of ontology construction. OntoClean modeling process starts by choosing the primitives that will represent each of the concepts based on metaproperties analysis. The metaproperties explicit concept relationship restrictions on the ontological level of knowledge, facilitating the identification of the concept through its rigidity, identity, unity and dependence. According to metaproperties set, restrictions are imposed on the construction of taxonomic ontology, facilitating to choose the correct constructs for representing and generate a model more cohesive with reality. Repair that in OntoClean ontology concepts can be described as properties.

The metaproperty rigidity can assume the values rigid, semi-rigid and anti-rigid, respectively represented by + R,-R and ~R. A property is classified as rigid if it is essential for all individuals who have it, or when if some individual ceases to own the property, it will also no longer cease to exist. For example, the property BE APE could be applied to primate individuals. An individual of that group, losing this essential property, could not exist, and therefore is characterized as a rigid property. However, the EAT BANANA property can be lost without affecting the individual and also may not be shared by everyone in the group, so it is not essential and therefore is classified as not rigid, in this case, semi-rigid. Semi-rigid properties are those essential for some of its individuals but not to others. Properties that are not essential for all its individuals are classified as anti-rigids. A taxonomic restriction imposed by this property is that rigid properties can not be a specialization (inheritance) of non-rigid properties. For example, the property BE APE can not specialize property BE CIRCUS MONKEY, since the latter is semi-rigid while the former is rigid. The individual who looses the property BE APE also cease to exist, while the individual who looses the property BE CIRCUS MONKEY will remain monkey. Thus, the correct specificitation is to model non rigid properties as specializations of rigid properties, to avoid inconsistencies.

The metaproperty identity is focused on the identification of a specific individual among other individuals. This is done by defining what characteristics make an individual unique. A concept/property can provide identity (+O) or just carry it (+I). For example, a PERSON provides identity (+O), but has a number of features that allow the distinction between another person. Meanwhile, a STUDENT does not provide identity, as it is provided by the PERSON which applies to student property. Therefore, STUDENT carries identity (+I) but not provide it. Properties are attributes that actually do not have any identity, as the property BEAUTIFUL, and have the label (-I). Just as rigidity, identity also restricts the taxonomy, preventing properties labeled (+I) are declared as specializations of properties labeled (-I), for instance, a PERSON can not be a subclass of BEAUTIFUL . Therefore, the notions of identity and rigidity are used to define the possibilities of hierarchical structure among represented objects, ensuring that only objects that share the same principles of identity belong to the same hierarchy. Thus, MAN and WOMAN are effectively subclasses of PERSON, because they carry identity for PERSON. However, STUDENT heritages the identity but can not be a specialization of the class.

The metaproperty unicity seeks to identify whether the object can be recognized from parts and boundaries. This is done by analyzing the composition of the object identifying whether it is a single or a sum of unitary objects. The set of conditions to determine if the properties have instances or individual unit is called the unicity criterion. The individuals whose properties are unitary and have the same unicity criterion are labeled (+ U). For example, individuals of BE A GRAIN OF SAND own label (+U) it is possible to identify the boundaries of the object. Individuals whose properties are unitary but have different criteria are labeled (-U) because they do not carry unicity. For example, the property BE QUADRUPED, may have different criteria for unicity among individuals, that is, each one may have a distinct unicity criterion. Properties of individuals that are not unitary are not labeled with (~U) because they carry anti-unicity. For example, BE (AN AMOUNT OF) SAND individuals has no unit as it is not possible to establish clear boundaries. This property also restrains the taxonomy such that (+U) properties can not specialize (-U) properties.

The metaproperty dependency identifies whether a concent/property is dependent on another. Properties with individuals that are dependent on individuals of another property to exist are labeled with (+D). Thus, it can be said that X may be externally dependent of a property Y. If this dependency does not exist, the property is labeled with (-D). For example, the MOM property can only exist if there is the OFFSPRING property, that is, one is externally dependent on the other. This property restricts the taxonomy preventing properties labeled (+D) to be specializations of properties labeled (-D).

1.2 Foundational Ontologies

A foundational ontology aims to establish a base to obtain consistency in the negotiations of meaning arised from the collaboration of individuals on a conceptual model [15]. Foundational ontologies have been used in the evaluation and (re)engineering process of modeling languages for describing conceptual categories that are used to build a concept that represents a certain part of reality.

The basis provided by the foundation brings advantages to modeling, guiding the construction of the knowledge model and helping to establish the taxonomic classification and relationships between the concepts. Thus, we obtain a reduction of ambiguity and an increase of the accuracy and consistency of the model. Therefore, we can create better anchored in reality models. We'll look at some concepts underlying the foundational ontology proposed by Guizzardi.

1.2.1 Isomorphism of Conceptual Models

According to Guizzardi [17], the conversational maximum for building conceptual models is that the message should be relevant full, clear, unambiguous, brief, without information excess and real through the point of view of the sender's knowledge. This is done by comparing the level of homomorphism between a concrete object of reality and its representation in a formal and explicit conceptualization. For this, we can analyze the properties that classify conceptual models isomorphism: Clarity, Correctness, Completeness and Laconicity. These properties will be used in this study and are therefore described below:

1.2.1.1 Lucidity

A specification (represented by constructs) S is called lucid in relation to a conceptual model M if a mapping (representation) from M to S is injective. A mapping from M to S is injective if and only if all entities of the specification S represent a maximum of one (or none) of the entity model M. Non-lucid diagrams occur when there is an

overload in the specification constructs, ie when more than one concept of the model map to the same construct, resulting in ambiguity.

1.2.1.2 Correction

A specification S is called correct in relation to a conceptual model if there is a surjective mapping (representation) from M to S. A
representation mapping from S to M is surjective if and only if the
mapping from S to the corresponding interpretation M is total, that is,
if and only if all the constructs of the specification S represents at
least one entity of M. Non-correct diagrams occur when there are
specification constructs that do not map to entities in conceptualizing, creating an excess of constructs.

1.2.1.3 Laconicity

A specification S is called laconic in relation to a conceptual model M if there is a mapping from S to M, which is injective, that is, if
and only if all the entities of M are represented by at most one (if
any) entity in representation S. Non-laconic diagrams occur when
there are concepts that are mapped to more than one construct in
the specification, generating redundancy constructs and unnecessary complexity to the representation.

1.2.1.4 Completeness

A specification S is called complete in relation to a conceptual
model M if there is a mapping from S to M that is surjective. A mapping from S to M is surjective if and only if the corresponding representation of the mapping from M to S is total, that is, if and only if all
the entities of the model are represented by at least one entity in

representation S. Incomplete diagrams occur when there are concepts that are not mapped to constructs, that is, there exists a lack of specification expressiveness to represent certain entities of conceptualization.

1.2.2 Unified Foundational Ontology

In 2005, a unified foundational ontology was proposed, which provides an ontological foundation for building conceptual models [16]. The Unified Foundational Ontology or UFO is divided into three fragments called UFO-A (Ontology of Endurants), UFO-B (Ontology of Perdurants) and UFO-C (Ontology of Social and Intentional Entities). The UFO-A defines the core of this ontology, providing a stable theory, formally characterized with the apparatus of a high expressiveness modal logic and possessing strong empirical support promoted by experiments in cognitive psychology [17]. The UFO-A introduces structural concepts about physical objects of reality to offer more semantics to conceptual modeling languages, which are described below.

Universals (Universals) represent high-level and abstract concepts that characterize different classes of individuals. Examples of Universal are: car, plane, plant, book, medical, weight. The Universal divide into Perdurant Universals and Endurant Universals.

Perdurant Universals represent concepts of individuals that are composed of temporal parts, they happen in time, extending over time and accumulating temporal parts, such as: race, storm, discussion, party.

Endurant Universals represent concepts of individuals that are always composed by its parts and that their identity does not vary over time. Endurant Universals fall into two classes, Moment Universals and Substantial Universals [17].

Moment Universals are concepts that exist only during the lifetime of any concrete individual. Examples of such universal are weight, height, length, feeling [17]. Substantial Universals represent individuals whose concepts are concrete, persist over time and keeps your identity, such as: person, car, cat, horse. These universals are also mutually independent, ie, the existence of one does not depend on another, except those who have essential partonomic relationships (relationships that condition the existence of an individual to the pre-existence of the other).

According to Guizzardi [17], Substantial Universal specialize into different categories, also seen as concepts metatypes, because they characterize with more precision the concepts of the ontology based on their metaproperties. They are:

Kind: represents the class of individuals whose instances are functional complexes. Example: person, dog, tree, chair, TV.

Subkind: represents the class of individuals who carry the rigid principle of identity provided by the concept of higher level (kind). Example: concept Man may be a subtype of the concept Person.

Phase: represents the partitioned classes of individuals in relation to a particular phase of existence. Example: Caterpillar and Butterfly are phases of the concept Lepdopterum.

Role: represents the class of individuals with a relational dependency of a kind, specifying the role it can play in the field. Example: Student (role) can be represented by the concept Person (kind).

Quantity: represents individuals who refer to portions of substances. These substances are related to language terms what refer to countless objects . Examples: land, water, salt, rock and yeast.

Category: classes of individuals representing different kind of type that share certain essential properties. Example: Being Alive category encompasses the concepts Animal and Person, both of type kind.

RoleMixin: represents distinct classes of individuals who share the type role certain essential properties. Example: Customer concept, of type RoleMixin, encompasses the concepts Student and Company, both of type role.

Mixin: represents classes of individuals in which some of its instances have essential properties while others have accidental properties. Example: SITTABLE mixin is a property that can be essential for CHAIR or COUCH, but accidental to STONE or BOX.

The hierarchy of Universals can be seen in Figure 1.1.

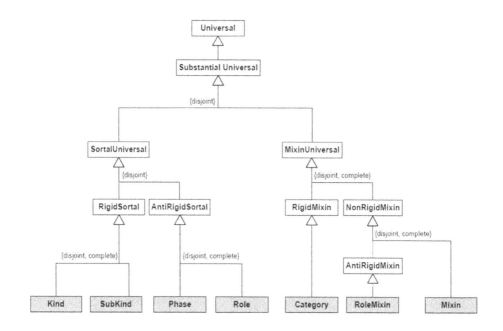

Figure 1.1 Hierarchy of metaconcepts of type Universal.

To facilitate the classification of the Substantial Universals, Guizzardi proposed a table that allows the identification of some major concepts metatypes from concepts metaproperties. These data can be seen in Table 1.2.

There are also the so-called Quality Universals and Mode Universals. The first refers to concepts that represent qualities and are inherent to a single individual, while the second refers to concepts that represent qualities but are incidental to other universals. For example, FEELING is a Mode Universal, while COLOR is a Quality Universal. Quality Universals are associated with one structure called Quality. Quality structures represent a set of possible values

(Qualia) that the Quality Universal can assume. For example, with the concept HEIGHT, the quality dimension which is the universal related is the set of positive real numbers. Each position in a quality dimension, or possible value is called a Quale [17].

Table 1.2 Table inference metatypes from metaproperties [17].

Category Type	Supply Identity (O)	Carry-Identity (I)	Rigidity (R)	Dependence (D)
SORTAL	-	+	+/-	+/-
Kind	+	+	+	-
SubKind	-	+	+	-
Role	-	+	-	+
Phase	-	+	-	-
NON-SORTAL	-	-	+/~	+/-
Category	-	-	+	-
RoleMixin	-	-	-	+
Mixin	-	-	~	-

The UFO-A has classifications for the relationships between concepts. In the foundational ontology, these relationships can be either material or formal. Formal relations occur between two entities directly, without any individual who relates them as "5 is greater than 3" or "this day is part of another month." Structural relations that express hierarchy (is-one), partonomy (part-of and its subtypes discussed in Chapter 4), among others are formal relations. Material Relations, on the other hand, have material structure itself and include examples such as jobs, kisses, air connections and commitments. These relations are intermediated by an individual who has the power to connect two entities, called Relator. For example, the relator EMPLOYMENT connects an EMPLOYEE with a COMPANY.

In this work, besides the interest in ontological foundation there is a strong interest in supporting visual domains. We decided to use the UFO-A for it provides the necessary constructs to work with the Substantial Universals, which are the objects that have visual representation, ie, concrete and visible objects.

The constructs proposed by Guizzardi guide the construction of the knowledge model, assisting in the taxonomic classification and in relationships establishment. Thus, it helps to decrease the occurrence of ambiguities and to increase the accuracy of the domain model.

1.3 Visual Knowledge

To understand what is visual knowledge, let's take a look at Lorenzatti's [26] definition:

"Visual Knowledge is the set of mental models (concepts) of real or imaginary scenes manipulated by the brain to handle tasks such as image-based interpretation or pattern or forms recognition in reality."

In other words, visual knowledge the set of mental models that support the process of reasoning over information from the visual aspects of the domain entities.

As we know, there are information areas where visual knowledge is a crucial part of the problem solving process. Areas such as Medicine, Biology, Engineering or Geology make constant use of visual components to facilitate the acquisition and dissemination of knowledge. If they were treated only in textual form, it would be very difficult to understand the parties. The Figure 1.2 shows, in order, images that display a tissue (biology), an x-ray (Medicine) and a rock structure (Geology).

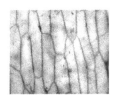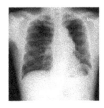

Figure 1.2 Examples of visual components in areas such as biology, medicine and geology, respectively.

In geology, for example, the expert analyzes visual information of rock formations to identify features and to correlate them with the occurrence of certain geological phenomena [1]. Therefore, the construction of ontologies in visual domains requires more than propositional descriptions to explain the concepts. This demand domain constructs to express specific content that can not be expressed textually.

By building alternative ontological models it is possible to represent visual knowledge in imagistic domains. Several previous approaches tried to capture the visual knowledge as neural networks, case-based foundational and image processing [25]. It is important to enlight that the focus of the acquisition and dissemination of visual knowledge is not in images, but in the mental model created by the expert to express the theory and practice acquired over the years.

You can extract the knowledge of experts through techniques of acquiring knowledge, but sharing it is often complicated because each individual creates his own mental model to reality. To understand this issue, we can analyze the Ullmann's triangle [17] which defines the relationship between an Object, a Concept and a Symbol. An Object can be found in reality but is dependent of the observer agent abstraction, a Concept is the internal mental representation created by the individual to abstract an object and a Symbol is a linguistic representation of the concept in a language. The symbol is an essential part of the triangle because it allows the externalization of knowledge and consequently its share among individuals of the same group.

When there is a lack of symbols to represent all aspects of a relevant concept, pictorial representations complement the symbolic representations. Thus, symbols and pictorial representations maintains a relationship with the concept being outsourced so that the pictorial representation anchor the symbol as shown in the Ullmann's triangle extension proposed by Lorenzatti and shown in Figure 1.3.

Icons are graphical representations that abstract non-relevant information to the process of visual recognition, omitting irrelevant aspects to the intention of the observer. An icon exclusively represent the concept, trying to avoid ambiguous or incorrect interpretations. Thus, the icons are perceptually similar to what they represent. Its meaning is captured through the same process of

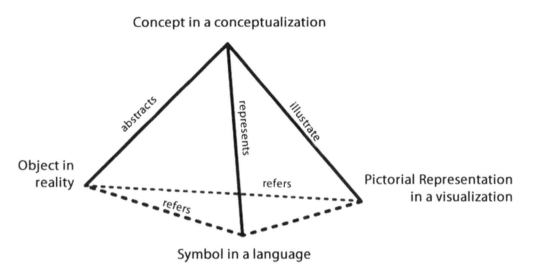

Figure 1.3 Extension of the triangle Ullmann considering the visual knowledge as a special kind of conceptualization that may have a symbolic or pictorial.

perception used to recognize the object or event. In other words, their meaning can be understood by observing the representation.

Images are photographs of concepts, which can be associated with the symbols of the language to provide examples of instances of a concept, supporting the explanation of their meaning.

This work studies how collaboration between members of a group can assist in obtaining a shared conceptualization better anchored in reality in imagistic domains where the dissemination of knowledge is more difficult due to lack of proper symbols to represent the visual aspects of modeled objects.

The application area is Sedimentary Stratigraphy, a sub-area of Geology that interprets the succession of deposits of sediments and their relationship to the geological time and generation process. The sedimentary deposits have enormous economic importance, since they define the conditions for the formation of the most important economic deposits such as gold, silver, coal and especially oil. The investigation of sedimentary deposits is made through the analysis of the rock type and spatial arrangement between the grains of this rock (called sedimentary structure), which define a unique visual aspect to each generating process and increases the probability of occurrences of deposits. The recognition and description of these aspects constitute the basic skill for mineral exploration.

In the next chapter we present some of the main existing methodologies for ontology engineering and construction, as well as basic concepts for the collaborative development of ontologies. Finally, we present a comparative evaluation of the main collaborative tools that represent the state of the art in this area.

2 ONTOLOGY ENGINEERING

The Ontology Engineering studies the activities involved in the ontology development, analyzing which methods of construction, management, manipulation and integration are involved in their life cycles. This area originated some methodologies that have the purpose of defining "what", "who" and "when" an activity should be performed. One method consists of different processes and each process is composed of activity which in turn may be one or more tasks. A task can be seen as the smallest unit of work in a process of building ontologies [10].

In order to allow geographically separated cooperative teams to interact during the build of ontologies, a process for ontology development was proposed [8] which is based on standards set by IEEE [22]. This process identifies what activities are involved in the construction of an ontology. As defined in [10], this process is divided into three distinct categories of activities:

Management activities of the ontology: includes schedule and task scheduling and auditing and quality control.

Activities oriented ontology development: divided into three stages, pre-development, development and post-development. The first stage is basically a *study of the environment*, evaluating platforms will use the ontology, which applications should be integrated, etc., and a feasibility study assessing whether it is possible to build the ontology. The second step involves the activities of *specification*, defining why and what are the intentions to build the ontology, *conceptualization*, structuring the domain of information with models of meaning in the knowledge level (Newell, 1982), *formalization*, transforming the conceptual model into a formal semi-computable model, and *implementation*, building computable models in a ontological language like OWL. In the final step, the activities involved with *maintance*, where the ontology is already can be used or reused by some applications.

Support activities: involve activities that occur in parallel to the development of the ontology, including the *knowledge acquisition*, focused on extracting the knowledge of experts in a given field or through automatic processes, *evaluation,* when a technical judgment of the ontology is made regarding software environment, *integration*, involving integration effort when the ontology is developed from pre-existing ontologies, *clustering*, when the ontology is developed from several pre-existing ontologies, *alignment*, when it is necessary to describe mappings between ontologies, *documentation*, clarifying implementation details and *configuration management*, storing records of all versions and documentation of the ontology along the development process.

The mentioned activities are addressed differently according to the chosen methodology for ontology engineering.

2.1 Collaborative Development of Ontologies

Sharing is one of the most basic goals of the concept of ontology. Reach the consensual knowledge in a group of people is needed to ensure that the generated model represents the portion of the world according to the viewpoint of the group, ie, there should not be the possibility of misinterpretation of the concepts and their relationships. Some recent applications use information sharing as a means of generating more content, such as Wikipedia (an encyclopedia built digital online: http://en.wikipedia.org). This idea relies heavily on using the web space as a space for participation. In fact, the use of emergent behavior is a trend known as Web 2.0, where individuals use their creativity sharing thoughts and collaborating [32].

The formalization of knowledge is one of the crucial steps in the process of knowledge engineering. We believe that using the phenomenon of collective collaboration as a tool to support the joint construction of ontologies is an evolution in relation to the construction of ontologies using traditional methodologies. Traditional methodologies are useful when we focus on a static, narrow and well defined domain. We know that, today, many information domains are dynamic and change all the time. Thus, the refinement of knowledge by users of different skills and viewpoints can play a critical role in obtaining a quality knowledge model. The joint use of methodologies for the creation of initial domain ontologies followed by a step of collaboration between domain experts may bring a more consistent result and converge more faster, avoiding long processes of knowledge extraction.

In this view, a collaborative environment that allows a group of people to develop a model of knowledge is the ideal tool for building consensus in dynamic domains. However, for this to occur, each member should be aware of modes of production and manipulation of knowledge [2].

Ideally, such a tool must be configurable to each organization, allowing changes to be made in the ontology, with workflows and processes and with a user interface that enables interaction through the cycle life of the system.

According to John & Melster [23], An environment for shared construction of knowledge models should:

(1) have a shared repository that enables common understanding, resource sharing and reuse of artifacts;

(2) allow people to create content in their own way, using their own terms and concepts;

(3) develop a map of top-down knowledge in the form of an ontology or concept map to help people define and structure their own concepts on a larger scale;

(4) allow the generation of knowledge, both bottom-up as top-down spontaneously and immediately.

Richards [32] completed this list of requirements, adding:

(5) support multiple levels of expertise, knowledge and visions of access rights;

(6) provide a review process in which users can register their approval or rejection;

(7) test and keep a record of consistency among elements of knowledge system, notifying users when conflicts arise;

(8) be compatible with a wide range of systems and sources of knowledge;

(9) provide a cycle intuitive, simple and well structured for maintaining knowledge;

(10) support editing of the knowledge model by domain users and not only by others, such as knowledge engineers;

(11) configurable, allowing changes in the ontology, the process of knowledge acquisition and system interface, along its life cycle.

2.1.1 Communication, Coordination and Cooperation

Groupware is a computer system that supports a group of users engaged in a common task or goal and that provides an interface to a shared environment. Thus, we can say that a system for collaborative ontology construction is a Groupware. This type of system demands strong interaction between the participants and usually requires well-defined user profiles and a shared environment accessible via the Internet. In our proposal, we built a tool Groupware focused on formalizing a domain ontology, through a well-defined collaborative. To support and formalize interactions in collaborative environment, we use as a conceptual basis for modeling the 3C Collaboration Model [9].

To collaborate, individuals must exchange information (communicate), organize (coordinate) and operate together in a shared space (to cooperate). The exchanges occurred during communication generate commitments that are managed by coordination, which in turn organizes and arranges the tasks that are performed in cooperation. By cooperating, individuals need to communicate, to renegotiate and to make decisions about situations not initially foreseen. This shows the cyclical aspect of collaboration. Through awareness, which is a process of acquiring information through the senses, an individual is informed about what is going on, what other people are doing and acquire information needed for his/her job [9].

In our proposal, we understand that to establish collaboration between users, some well-defined roles are needed to maintain the organization of data and stimulate the motivation of the group in the environment. There are three well-defined roles: Domain Experts,

Engineers Knowledge and Visitors. Domain experts should be able to propose changes in the ontology elements. Knowledge engineers can make changes that bring more formalize the model and to propose issues to experts warn or ban users with bad behavior. Visitors should be able to act freely in the environment without making any change in the knowledge model.

All types of users must have permission to write comments about ontology elements (this kind of comment is also called "annotation"), generating discussion.

In conclusion, access to the built environment conference should be made available to users, providing negotiation and progressive refinement of definitions and concepts for structuring the design community until a consolidated model is obtained.

2.1.2 Collaborative Ontology Development Tools

Recently, the focus of tools for building ontologies have been collaboration. As we have seen, the fields of information are very dynamic, requiring many opinions to form a common vocabulary. The following are some of the main tools for building ontologies that address aspects of collaboration to build knowledge models.

2.1.2.1 Collaborative Protégé - Stanford University

The Protégé is one of the leading ontology editors, consisting of an open source project. Its knowledge base framework was developed by Stanford Medical Informatics. This framework allows the representation of knowledge in different formalisms as the traditional frames and newer languages such as RDF and OWL. Collaborative Protégé introduced features to allow collaborative building among users. The system is based on client-server architecture, where multiple users can simultaneously edit the ontology [27].

Collaborative Protégé allows users to comment on the components of the ontology, discuss changes and reach consensus interactively through modeling decisions. This is controlled by recording notes and changes made on the components of the ontology. Among the features provided by the system include:

- Annotation ontology elements such as classes, properties and instances
- Annotation of ontology changes as class creation, deletion, change of name, etc..
- Support for proposed changes and proposed vote
- Support for filtering existing notes
- Support for chat

An interesting aspect of the tool is that it used metadata of ontologies to guide the collaborative interaction. Tudorache's work [35] proposed a meta ontology CHAO (Change and Annotation Ontology) to provide constructs that represent the components of the domain ontology, changes and annotations made in the ontology and the different types of users. Thus, the tool creates instances of this metaontology to represent changes made on the domain ontology.

However, the tool does not support ontological foundation or visual domains and need some prior knowledge in OWL or other representation formalism is required to properly build an ontology, because the interface is oriented to formal language constructs.

2.1.2.2 NeOn Toolkit

The NeOn Toolkit is a multi-platform ontology engineering tool. Based on a methodology of ontology construction, the environment seeks to provide understanding and support for the whole development cycle of an ontology. The tool has a modular architecture, providing features such as ontology repository, distributed components, inference and collaboration. The focus of the tool is the support to the life cycle of ontology [19].

The target community of the NeOn Toolkit includes researchers from the semantic web, knowledge management and related areas, as well as market professionals.

The environment is heavily based on plugins that add functionality to the system. The plugin discussion Cicero [7] allows ontology elements and associated changes have discussions in a more organized. The main idea is to provide an environment that supports collaboration in a larger community.

2.1.2.3 WebODE

The environment WebODE [3] focuses on the entire life cycle of ontology, providing not only collaboration features, but also providing a scalable infrastructure for the development of other ontology development tools or applications based on ontologies.

The WebODE is not just a development environment, but a complete structure with various services related to ontology, focused on fulfilling needs of current tools for deepening the acceptance of the use of ontologies in the business.

The tool allows the collaboration at the level of knowledge, possessing resources to avoid problems of concurrent editing. However, collaboration is not the focus of the environment and is partially addressed by not allowing the visualization of the collaboration history or use of notes linked to the ontology.

The WebODE allows you to perform a post-processing of the ontology, using the methodology OntoClean to identify incorrect hierarchical relationships (is-a).

2.1.2.4 OntoEdit

OntoEdit [34] is an environment for ontology engineering, which focuses on combining the ontology development methodologies based on the ability to collaborate and inference.

According to the methodology, the OntoEdit is based on three main steps for developing ontologies: requirements specification, refinement, and evaluation. The requirements for the construction of ontology are collected from knowledge engineers and domain experts in a joint effort to describe the domain ontology. This step generates a semi-formal description of ontology as output. The refinement phase extends this semi-formal description through several iterations, formalizing the ontology in a representation language. This phase generates as output an ontology more mature, already formalized. After the third phase, the evaluation seeks to assess the ontology according to the requirements that were specified in the first phase. This phase validates the developed ontology is useful to the team of knowledge engineers and users also target ontology or application that uses. This phase generates as output a validated ontology, ready to go into a productive environment.

In the current version of the system, support for collaborative development, which seeks to meet the needs arising from conflicts generated by the joint construction of the ontology. Clients connect to the server, which has the global version of the ontology. Customers are immediately informed of any changes to the global template.

Likewise the WebODE the OntoEdit also provides the post-processing functionality of the ontology using the methodology to identify incorrect OntoClean hierarchy relationships (is-a).

2.1.2.5 Fabrico

Manufacturing Environment [29] was developed by researchers at UFRGS and aims to provide an operating environment in which Web 2.0 for lecturers, researchers and students collaboratively develop information science through fragments of texts published in various formats. These fragments are organized through metadata-based ontologies and produced by members of the community. Thus, the environment can be seen as directed towards the Semantic Web.

The tool consists of several features, quote: extractor text snippets web, document repository, collaborative writing environment (wiki) system folksonomies, annotation system based on thesaurus and bookmark system. Through these tools, community members produce wiki texts, record the documents produced, generate records of web bookmarks, describe content according to a thesaurus and define descriptors (keywords or tags) for such content. However, Oliveira et al. [29] shows how the system can also be used for collaborative construction of ontologies.

Fabrico focuses on leveraging and disseminating information and knowledge related to a particular degree course, allowing it to be formally described and disseminated through the collaborative construction of information. The tool is therefore a collaborative environment that seeks to categorize information through metadata. Thus, the collaboration stage output is structured information according to metadata.

2.1.3 Evaluation Metrics

To perform an analysis of the tools, we developed some defined criteria for comparison, assuming the need to permit the collaborative construction of ontologies using foundational constructs ontological and pictorial components for visual domains. Thus, we selected criteria related to collaboration features, functionality, web systems, and support for ontological foundation support visual domains:

a) **Structured Discussion (Notes)**

   Ability of users to view other comments and discuss among themselves issues relevant to collaboration, forming opinions and motivating new changes in the ontology.

b) **History of Collaboration**

   Storage and querying the history of changes made to the domain ontology,

c) **Support for OWL**

   Ability to import and export the domain ontology in OWL, enabling the exchange of data with other systems.

d) **Support the Inference**

   Mechanisms to perform automated foundational on the domain ontology, through the constraints of meaning entered by users.

e) Detection of Inconsistencies

Ability to detect conflicts and inconsistencies in the domain ontology.

f) Distinct User Profiles

Support for user groups with different features and access permissions to system functionality.

g) Intuitive Web Interface

User interface of the system with proper usability to all users.

h) Centralized Access via Web Browser

Access to unique system through a web browser and not by installing desktop software.

i) Allows use without previous knowledge of formal ontology

Ability of users to use the tool, changing the domain ontology even without prior knowledge of formal ontology, ie, the interface should use common terms and easy to understand by the user.

j) Use in Visual Domains

Capacity of building ontologies for visual domains, with the addition of icons and photographs related to ontology elements.

k) Using the methodology OntoClean

Using the OntoClean methodology for taxonomic validation and ontological metaproperties classification, within the context of collaboration.

l) Use of Ontological Foundation

Using primitive ontological foundation to enrich the classification of concepts, properties and relations.

The tools were classified according to media that comes to each of the criteria. Tools that implement enough features to meet the criteria were classified as "YES", as tools that lack or have insufficient functionality to meet the criteria were classified as "NO". The comparative table of the tools described in this chapter is presented in Table 2.1.

Table 2.1 Comparative table of the tools of collaborative construction of ontologies.

Criterion	Manufac-turing	OntoEdit	NeOn Toolkit	Collaborative Protégé	WebODE
Structured Discussion (Notes)	NO	NO	YES	YES	NO
History of Collaboration	NO	NO	NO	YES	NO
Support for OWL	NO	NO	YES	YES	YES
Support the Inference	NO	YES	YES	YES	YES
Detection of Inconsist-encies	NO	YES	YES	YES	YES
Distinct User Profiles	NO	NO	NO	NO	NO
Intuitive Web Interface	YES	NO	NO	YES	NO
Centralized Access via Web Browser	YES	YES	NO	YES	YES
Allows use without pre-vious knowledge of formal ontology	YES	YES	YES	NO	NO
Use in Visual Domain	NO	NO	NO	NO	NO
Using the methodology OntoClean	NO	YES	NO	NO	YES
Use of Ontological Foundation	NO	NO	NO	NO	NO

Analyzing the tools, we concluded that most of them do not pro-vide enough constructs to capture more complete semantics, ie, do not have enough precision to specify the knowledge in its completeness and may generate incomplete models (as seen in section 1.2.1).

This lack of constructs also complicates the discussion of meaning, since often the concepts are not modeled avoiding ambiguity and redundancy. Moreover, many of these tools are also oriented to representation of formal languages, such as OWL, so as the interface. This complicates the use of the tool by users who do not have this expertise.

Research done in the area of collaborative ontology not only witnessed the fact that collaborative authoring ontologies strengthens the process of ontology engineering, but also indicated that the development and improvement of collaborative ontology is not well served by any of the current tools for authoring ontologies [27]. Moreover, current tools also do not include Ontological Foundation and Visual Domains.

An important aspect is that the tools do not provide adequate support to the problem of ontological choice, ie, how to best represent the primitive concept analysis in order to create better models anchored in reality. The weak correction laconicity and clarity of representation languages ontologies enable the production of a variety of specifications of the same conceptual model and subsequent interpretations of these different models for different information users. The use of metadata based on foundational ontologies guides the choice of representations and allows a reduction of variations in the model specification. It is considered that more uniform models are equally and evenly interpreted.

Likewise, the sharing of vocabularies is increasingly associated with the use of images and visual constructs, for the dissemination of image capture equipments and distribution of images in digital media. The actual construction of the concept in the mind of the sender is strongly grounded in visual knowledge, whose treatment is still incipient in the analysed ontology construction tools.

Interactive systems should not be limited to its usefulness, but also ensure that it is provided in an agile way. Two aspects should be taken into account: if no collaborative environment is provided for the development of ontologies, the ontologies produced are not a product of a social process. On the other hand, if the tool does not provide good usability, the process of ontology engineering can not wait to spread their ideas for a non-specialist audience [21]

In the next chapter we present the architecture of the knowledge model based on metadata, which underlies the collaborative environment through metaontologies formalizing the representation of ontological constructs and the structure of the collaboration.

3 MODELING

The main motivation for this work arose from the existence of great difficulty in sharing formal knowledge among experts. Geographical distances and understanding barriers often prevent the obtainance of consensus on a specific area, even after an efficient knowledge extraction. The development of ontologies is time consuming, expensive and involves highly specialized professionals. Consequently, the process needs to be optimized in order to achieve lower development costs and to cope with the amount of information with which we live today.

Based on this, we noticed a shortage in the area of Knowledge Engineering for a tool for collaborative construction of ontologies to support visual domains and ontological foundation, which allow the experts and knowledge engineers to cooperate intuitively about a certain domain of information on the web, generating domain ontologies with appropriate representation. Ie, we have developed an online system for collaborative development of ontologies, focusing on specifying ontologies that allow more expressiveness and precision through better organized constructs with support to ontological foundation and visual knowledge.

In our work, the basic ontological components (concept, property and relation), were extended according to the foundational ontology UFO-A, which allow their specialization with richer constructs, increasing the expressiveness of the model, reducing ambiguities and facilitating taxonomic classification. Additionally, the use of constructs and visual components allows experts to anchor the symbolic knowledge of pictorial form, clarifying and facilitating the sharing of information among users of the system, especially in visual fields as Geology and Medicine.

For best results, we looked at aspects of existing collaboration systems or groupwares, aiming to build a truly effective tool in the process of domain ontologies building via an easy to use interface, with intuitive buttons and functions.

Based on these requirements, we modeled a collaborative environment conceptually based on metadata in the form of higher level ontologies to define the structure of the collaboration (referred here as metaontologies), where the desired expressiveness and precision are met through the use of foundational ontology constructs and visual knowledge.

3.1 Metadata Structure

Metadata are usually described in the literature as information about information, but are actually structured information that describe, explain, find or help in the recovery or management of any information resource [31]. A metadata record contains pre-defined elements representing specific attributes of a resource asset, with each one having one or more attribute values. Metadata provide a more systematic way to categorize information through informative statements about a particular type of data. However, to efficiently retrieve the information, the data need to be stored properly, allowing controls to reduce ambiguities and redundancies. Thus, we can use controlled vocabularies, taxonomies, thesauri and ontologies.

In this work, we constructed a model of knowledge in a metadata layer, which underlies the entire collaborative application, defining the elements manipulated by the system and the users. The knowledge model has two distinct goals: representing the domain representation ontology and collaboration. The proposed model specifies metaconstructs, enabling the system to understand the components of the domain ontology, manipulating them properly and recording the changes during the collaboration process.

The knowledge model uses the concepts of two higher-level ontologies developed to allow manipulation of ontological objects in a collaborative environment:

Representation Ontology: specifies the structure of the components of the domain ontology.

Collaboration Ontology: specifies the structure of the collaboration components in order to obtain a consensual and shared conceptualization.

These metaontologies structure the manipulation of the ontological objects of the domain ontology. The domain ontology specifies the domain structure in the form of concepts, properties and relations with accurate constructs. This ontology is the main manipulated artifact and any change on it is done through instantiating concepts of the defined metaontologies.

Both metaontologies constructs provide support for ontological foundation and visual knowledge in order to achieve better completeness in domain ontologies generated by the system. Next, the use of metaontologies is explained in detail.

3.2 Modeling Collaboration with Metaontologies

The ontological modeling focuses on identifying the concepts of a domain and specifying them in an ontology using a specification language based on domain independent ontological categories (also called upper-level ontologies or top ontologies) [18].

In this work, we introduce an ontology with top independent domain metadata to specify the components of the domain ontology and collaboration events. Our main contribution was to develop a metadata layer that allows to build an ontology of the domain in a language-independent representation, but incorporating elements of foundational ontology UFO-A and providing support visual domains. Thus, specific constructs were created to provide more precision to the domain ontology, which are built through the following questions:

a) which components of the ontology should be represented and with what structure?

b) which of these components of the ontology may be seen as collaborative objects by users?

c) which collaboration events should be represented and with what structure?

A collaboration event occurs from the user interaction with the system. It may be a change in any component of the domain ontology or an annotation (comment, question, answer, etc..) on some component of the domain ontology. The set of changes is stored in a structured manner to allow the mapping of the evolution of ontology extraction and intermediate models during the various interactions that are made in the collaborative process to obtain a shared conceptualization.

The collaborative system is structured into three distinct layers: conceptual, metadata and data. The conceptual layer is not implemented, but serves as an ontological basis for the other layers. As we saw earlier, the system works with three ontologies (two metaontologies and domain ontology). The domain ontology is manipulated directly by users and is located in the data layer as it contains data entered by the active collaboration community. The Representation and Collaboration metaontologies are part of the metadata layer, structuring the domain ontology and collaboration respectively. Both have accurate and meaningful constructs because they are based on the foundational ontology UFO-A [16], which is part of the conceptual layer. The complete structure of the ontologies involved in the process of collaboration can be seen in Figure 3.1.

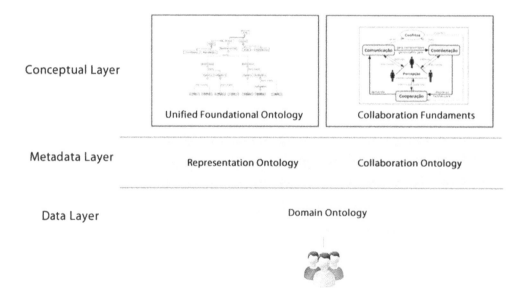

Figure 3.1 Structure of the ontology collaboration system.

Importantly, the system user directly manipulates only the domain ontology, ie the metaontology Representation and collaboration are not the object of collaboration, they are used for the purpose of organizing and structuring information, acting only in the layer base system.

The Representation Ontology defines what can be created in the domain ontology, while Collaboration Ontology defines what can be changed in the domain ontology. In other words, R.O. defines ontological components as "concept", "property" and "Relationship" while the C.O. events defines collaboration as "Concept Created", " Property Deleted" and "Value Created", for example.

In this structure, the domain ontology is created by instantiating the ontology of representation, as well as the history of collaboration (set of events changes made on the domain ontology) is created by instantiating the collaboration ontology. For example: Representation Ontology has a metaconcept called "Concept" while the Collaboration Ontology has a metaconcept called "Concept Created". When a user uses the system to create a new concept in the Domain Ontology, this concept should be inserted in the Domain Ontology and creation event should be recorded in the history of collaboration. This is done by creating an instance of the metaconcept "concept" and an instance of metaconcept "Concept Created", generating the necessary records to represent the domain ontology and collaborative activity performed. The structure of interaction between metadata ontologies and their instances can be seen in Figure 3.2.

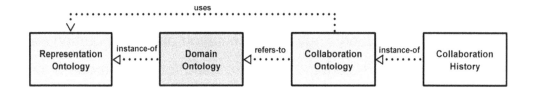

Figure 3.2 Structure of metadata ontologies and their instances.

Below, we detail the proposed Representation and Collaboration metaontologies.

3.2.1 Representation Ontology

To allow the definition of domain ontologies, we proposed a highest level ontology metadata to distinguish the components of the ontology and to represent them so that computer systems can understand and manipulate that data. We focused on a simplified representation by providing specific constructs to each element of the ontology, using metadata to represent the domain model and maintain the end user away from any representation formalisms.

When dealing with ontology, we seek to represent their basic constructs: concepts, describing objects of reality, Properties, describing attributes that characterize concepts and relations, describing mappings between relational concepts. In this work we are interested in expanding the set of basic constructs, providing more expressive and constructs that allow:

- representation of the basic ontological constructs;

- The use of pictorial representations, allowing visual representation of domains [26] by association of images and icons to concepts and properties;

- metaproperties using concepts defined in the methodology OntoClean [12];

- the use of the concepts and relationships metatypes partonomic defined in UFO-A [17];

-

By using the visual concepts and constructs in the environment, it is possible to associate a concept with an icon or one or more images, beyond the traditional symbolic representation through a linguistic term, as can be seen in Figure 3.3.

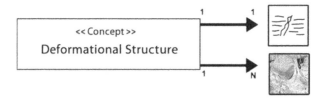

Figure 3.3 Association of visual constructs to a concept.

Properties that have a set of defined values can also have associated to each value, an icon representing it. For example, the property Rounding present in ontology Sedimentary Stratigraphy (Geology) has three defined values: sub-rounded, rounded, well rounded. Each value can have a visual anchoring via an icon, as seen in Figure 3.4.

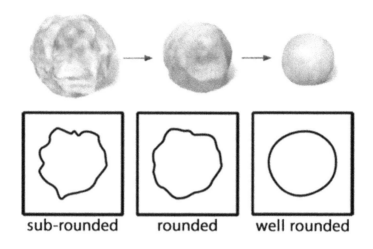

sub-rounded   rounded   well rounded

Figure 3.4 Association of visual constructs to property values.

Additionally, we selected constructs of UFO-A looking to equate the level of specialization semantics with the interaction ability of the user with these constructs. As we focused in the field of interest of sedimentary stratigraphy (which is composed basicly of concrete objects), some constructs as Time Universal was not used in this work. Among the selected constructs are:

- the concepts metatypes defined as subclasses of the Substantial Universal: sortal, kind, subkind, quantity, etc..
- properties: quality universal properties
- partonomic relationships: component-of ,-member of, etc.

These constructs, if used in the correct manner, impose semantic constraints on the model, helping users to detect meaning faults and representation errors in the domain ontology.

The R.O. describes the structural components of the domain ontology (concept, property, relations, etc..), representing them through his concepts. Therefore, the root concept of this ontology is OntologyComponent having as sub-concepts OntologyConcept, OntologyProperty, OntologyPropertyValue, OntologyRelation, OntologyImage and OntologyConceptMetaProperty, which respectively represent the objects Concept, Property, Property Value, Value, Image and metaproperty Concept (originated from OntoClean).

The Representation Ontology defines how the application interprets the ontological components, helping the collaborative system to detect whether they were correctly defined by users. Therefore, the domain ontology created by users is formalized in terms of representation ontology by instantiating its concepts. To illustrate, a concept domain hypothetical Rock would be represented as an instance of metaconcept RigidSortal, a subclass of the metaconcept OntologyConcept (seen right below). Similarly, a domain property Angularity would be represented as an instance of metaconcept OntologyProperty, as well as the relationship compostaPor would be represented as an instance of metaconcept OntologyRelation. The (meta) Representation Ontology concepts have their own properties, which need to be assigned at the time of instantiation.

We assume that all the concepts of Representation Ontology possess two properties to represent the linguistic symbol in each language. They are implemented as text values (string): labelEN to English and Portuguese is labelPT. More properties can be added to support other languages.

To provide visual support, we use the metaconcept Ontolo-gyImage, which is specialized in two sub-concepts: Photography (to represent photographs of bodies and Icon (to represent symbolic pictorial icons [26]. The R.O. contains some relations that connect the metaconcept OntologyConcept the metaconcept Icon, allowing the connection of up to an icon, and the metaconcept Photography, allowing the bond of photographs. These artifacts correspond to the connection between a concept and its pictorial representation, de-scribed in Ullmann's triangle.

To add ontological foundation to the model, some of the meta-concepts of Representation Ontology were specialized in some of the constructs proposed bu the foundational ontology UFO-A [16].

In this work we focus on representing only the concrete entities of the world, because the domain ontology used for validation (Sedi-mentary Stratigraphy) mainly represents that object type. Guizzardi proposed a hierarchy of that object type, called the Substantial Uni-versal [17]. The types of these are also described as Universal metatypes concepts. Using these metatypes, it is possible to repre-sent a concept of ontology constructs that best represent their rela-tionship with reality.

With mentioned in section 1.2, the methodology OntoClean [12] examines the concepts of a domain in terms of how they relate in reality. The OntoClean starts the modeling process by choosing the primitives that will represent each of the concepts based on metap-roperties analysis. The metaproperties seek explicit restrictions on the ontological level of knowledge, facilitating the identification of the concept through its essence, identity, unicity and dependence. The use of metaproperties helps create more robust models, especially if used in conjunction with a foundational ontology.

For purposes of interaction with the user, specify the identity metaproperty dividing it into two loads provides identity and identity. The others are directly mapped to the concepts of Representation Ontology. Thus, the metaconcept OntologyConceptMetaProperty was specialized with the possible metaproperties described in OntoClean. We define metaproperties and their possible values as below:

Rigidity: Rigid (+R), Semi-Rigid (-R), Anti-Rigid (~R)

Dependence: Dependent (+D), Non-Dependent (-D)

SupplyIdentity: Provides (+O), Don't Provide (-O)

CarryIdentity: Loads (+I), No Load (-I)

Unity: Unit (+U), No Unit (-U) Anti-Unit (~U)

In order to provide for the construction of an ontology more precise, the relationships established in the table described in section 1.3.2 were incorporated into the system to make it possible to infer the concept metatype from the classification of its metaproperties. Thus, the expert user can interact directly with the metaproperties, which are easier to classify than metatypes, for those who do not possess consolidated knowledge on ontological foundation. The classification of metatypes requires prior and depth knowledge of UFO-A. As users of the system will not have this a priori knowledge, understanding and classification of metaproperties is sufficient for the system to assign the appropriate metatypes concepts. Thus, we believe that this aspect of foundational in the domain ontology occur naturally and with little or no interference from the knowledge engineer, as seen in Figure 3.5.

Following Guizzardi's idea, properties are defined as Quality Universals. Quality Universals are associated with Quality Structures. Therefore, the metaconcept OntologyProperty has been specialized in QualityStructure and this was specialized in QualityDimension. Quality Structures represent a set of possible values (Qualia) that the property can take. Each position in a quality dimension or possible value is called Quale [17]. Thus, a quality structure has one or more Quales. Some structures may have a well-defined set of values, such as HIGH, MEDIUM, LOW, others may be related to an infinite

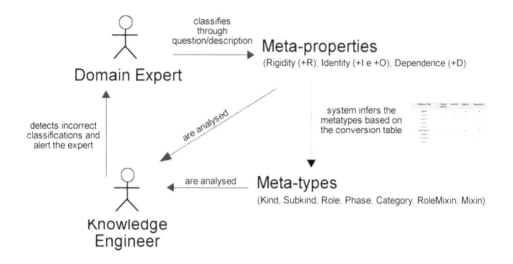

Figure 3.5 Interaction with the expert metaproperties to infer concept metatype.

As we have seen, the relations in UFO-A can be either material or formal. The part-whole relationships are formal, as well as the reporting relationship between two concepts, also called "subsumption" or "is-a" is also a formal relationship. The part-whole relationships are classified in relation to the types of individuals that connect and are divided into four types: subQuantityOf, which relates individuals that are quantities (Quantity metatype) subCollectionOf, which relates individuals that are collective (metatype Collective) memberOf, which lists individuals who are functional complexes (Kind metatype) and componentOf or collective, which lists individuals who are functional complexes. The material relations are mediated by an individual who has the power to connect two entities.

These specializations increase the expressiveness of the generated models as constructs are more accurate to describe the objects of the domain ontology. The classification based concepts, properties and relations avoids ambiguity, modeling errors and facilitates ontological choices that occur at each step of the collaboration. Through these more accurate constructs, the real meaning of ontological objects can be inferred from their rating by users, generating a well foundated domain ontology at the end of the collaborative process. Based on all these definitions, the complete Representation Ontology can be seen in Figure 3.6.

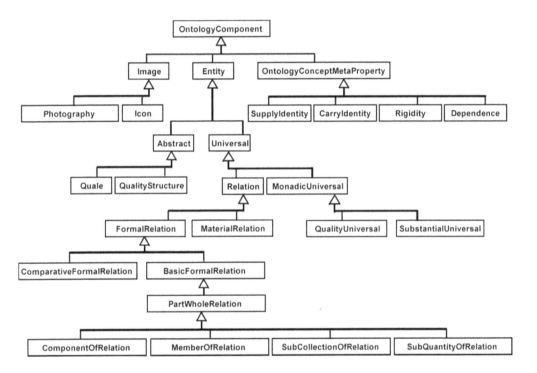

Figure 3.6 Full taxonomy of the Representation Ontology.

3.2.2 Collaboration Ontology

The Collaboration Ontology (C.O.) defines which collaborative activities can be done in the domain ontology. The collaboration process is focused on managing and storing changes made on concepts, properties and relationships and also annotations linked to the components of the ontology. Through the web application, the experts can create changes or annotations directly on the domain model, adding, changing or removing components of the ontology. Collaboratively, they can see the history of changes of other users and discuss about them through the notes, while making new changes when necessary until they get a consolidated domain model.

Internally, the application stores the collaboration events by instantiating the concepts of the Collaboration Ontology. These concepts are important metadata to define the set of possible modifications in the domain ontology. A change event (instance of C.O.) has properties that define its meaning: *domainComponent* relates the change to a component of the domain ontology; *author* stores the username of who made the change, *date* stores the date and time when the change occurred, *value* stores the new user-defined value for the component (new name, property value, etc..); *language* stores the language in which the property value is. The C.O. concepts describe the collaboration events, which are divided into Change and Annotation.

We can see the key concepts of the Collaboration Ontology (without their specializations) in Figure 3.7 and further we explain in detail how each collaboration event was modeled.

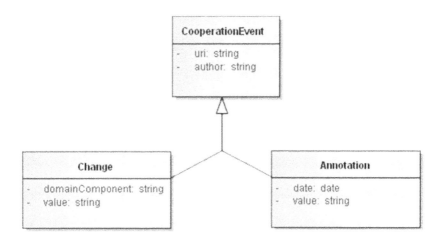

Figure 3.7 High-level structure in Collaboration Ontology.

3.2.2.1 Changes Modeling

A change can occur in a concept, a property, a property value, a relation or a term (language symbol). Therefore, the metaconcept Change was specialized as shown in Figure 3.8.

Figure 3.8 Specialization of the concept of change Change.

We will now detail each of the possible changes in the system. The change in terms of components is done using the metaconcept LabelChange. The other specializations require changes to allow a full crawl of the collaborative activities.

To represent changes involving concepts, we specialize the met-aconcept ConceptChange as shown in Figure 3.9.

Figure 3.9 Specialization of metaconcept ConceptChange for changes in concepts.

Thus, the change events that are related to some concept of domain ontology are:

- ***ConceptCreated*** : Creating a new concept or sub-concept;
- ***ConceptIconChange*** *:* change icon pictorial concept;
- ***ConceptPhotographyChange*** : Change one of the photos of instances of the concept. It is possible to add a new photo (ConceptPhotographtCreated) or delete an existing photo (conceptPhotographyRemoved);

70

- ***ConceptPropertyCreated*** : Creation of a property in the ontology related with the concept in question;
- ***ConceptPropertyRemoved*** : Removal of a property related with the concept of ontology in question;
- ***ConceptRelationCreated*** : Creation of a relation related with the concept in question;
- ***ConceptRelationRemoved*** : Removal of a relation related to the concept in question;
- ***ConceptRemoved***: Removal of the concept in question.
- ***ConceptTypeChange***: Metatype change in the concept;
- ***ConceptMetaPropertyChange*** : Changing the value of one of metaproperties concept, classified ConceptSupplyIdentityChange, ConceptCarryIdentityChange, ConceptDependeceChange, ConceptRigidityChange or ConceptUnityChange;

We can also introduce the following changes on properties:

- ***PropertyCreated*** : creation a new property in the ontology;
- ***PropertyRemoved*** : removal of a property of the ontology;
- ***PropertyTypeChange*** : change of the type of property value (domain), for example, integers (int), text (string), real (float) or predefined values (qualia);

In the case of properties which have a finite set of values and predefined specialize a type-specific change of the set value, as seen in Figure 3.10, each value of the set of values (Qualia) property is called Quale by UFO-A, as seen in the previous chapters.

Figure 3.10 Specialization of metaconcept PropertyValueChange for changes in property values.

The following changes may occur with property values:

- **PropertyValueCreated** : creation of a new value of the property;
- **PropertyValueRemoved** : removal of a property value;
- **PropertyValueIconChanged** : icon changes related to property value;

The hierarchical relationship IS-A is treated as a formal non-differentiated relation. Although there is abundant material in the literature on semantic subtypes with distinct taxonomic relations, it was not addressed in this work because it is a structuring relation.

We can introduce the following changes on relations:

- **RelationCreated** : creation of a new relation in the ontology, specialized in the following metaconcepts for better tracking of which relationship was created:
  - ○ **FormalRelationCreated** : direct relations
    - ▪ **SubClassOfRelationCreated** : hierarchical relationships
    - ▪ **PartOfRelationCreated** : partonomic relations

- *MemberOfRelationCreated*
- *SubQuantityOfRelationCreated*
- *SubCollectionOfRelationCreated*
- *ComponentOfRelationCreated*
  - *MaterialRelationCreated* : relationships with intermediar (relator)

- *RelationRemoved* : removal of a relation of the ontology;
- *RelationSourceCardinalityChange* : changing the value of the origin concept cardinality [0 .. 1, 0 .. n, 1 .. n, 1];
- *RelationTargetCardinalityChange* : changing the value of the origin concept cardinality [0 .. 1, 0 .. n, 1 .. n, 1];
- *RelationTargetConcept* : changing the value of the target concept cardinality;
- *RelationTypeChange*: changing the type of relationship, for example, from Formal to Material, from MemberOf to SubCollection, etc..

Finally, we have built a framework that enables the creation of elements in the domain ontology through the instantiation of metaconcepts in a specific metadata layer. This layer provides visual components required for collaborative visual domains and components with well-defined semantics necessary for the application of ontological foundation in the process of collaboration. An example that shows a complete picture of collaboration architecture can be seen in Figure 3.11.

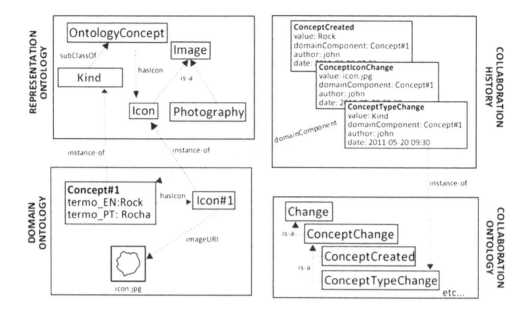

Figure 3.11 Example of collaboration structure with visual constructs and foundational.

In this figure, we see a series of three collaboration activities: ConceptCreated, ConceptIconChange and ConceptTypeChange. The creation of the concept "Rock" generated a record of this event in Collaboration History (new instance of the metaconcept Concept-Created of the Collaboration Ontology) and a new component in the domain ontology, Concept # 1 (which is an instance of the metaconcept OntologyConcept of the Representation Ontology). After, a change was made on concept icon, indicating that the new icon is "icon.jpg". Likewise, there was created an instance of the metaconcept Icon of the Representation Ontology, generating the component domain Icon # 1, linked to image "icon.jpg", and an instance of the metaconcept ConceptIconChange of the Collaboration Ontology,

74

generating the record of this event in history. Finally, we made a change in the concept metatype through the instantiation of the metaconcept ConceptTypeChange of the Collaboration Ontology, which indicates that the concept is not an instance of OntologyConcept anymore, but an instance of one of its specializations, the Kind. This is one of the major changes in the environment, as it allows the concept to be defined in terms of more precise constructs as defined in UFO-A. At first, concepts can be specified more generally, using the construct OntologyConcept, and later be changed to more specific semantics, specializing as one of the possible metatypes: Kind, Role, Quantity, Collective, etc..

3.2.2.2 Annotations Modeling

As previously mentioned, users can discuss among themselves and generate feedback on the components of the ontology through annotations.

IBIS (Issue-based Information System) is an argumentation method and has the objective to support the coordination and planning of policy decisions processes by identifying, structuring and defining the issues arised out of the problem solving groups, and also to provide relevant information to speech [24]. The methodology IBIS provides the following elements to construct the argument:

Issue: defines a new discussion topic from a conceptual perspective.

Idea: answers a question and refers the formalization in the conceptual view.

Justification: arguments related to an issue or idea. They can be of type Evaluation, to provide measures or experiments or Example, to increase the confidence of the argument.

Challenge: arguments against an issue or idea, divided into Counter-Example, providing a counter-example and Alternative, providing a comparison.

Although models of argumentation provide a conceptual model for the interaction of issues, ideas and arguments, they do not accurately differentiate the distinct types of arguments that arise in a discussion originated from a knowledge engineering collaborative process. In our work, we propose a communication model based on the concepts of IBIS methodology, but without the commitment to use the nomenclature or semantics of existing elements. Thus, we introduce different elements and relationships between them to compose the discussion in a collaborative environment for building ontologies. However, some of the elements in our model can be seen as equivalent to the elements of IBIS.

In the developed application, we have built a structure of annotations seeking to increase the traceability of decisions on the conceptual model through the creation of argumentative components with links to the domain ontology components or with changes made to the ontology.

In our metadata model, an annotation is a specialization of the metaconcept of CooperationEvent (from Collaboration Ontology). An annotation is a comment about some artifact of the environment, be it a component of the ontology (concept, property, relation), a change event or even another annotation.

To identify the discussion semantics and avoid the arguments to consist only of plain text related to the artifacts ontology, we proposed specific annotation subtypes with semantic relations between them, allowing to extract more information and to relate the events of collaboration, shown as Figure 3.12. The relationship ApplyTo connects the annotation with the object to which the annotation is applied. These links allow a structured discussion, linking the interactions and creating a network of inter-related conversation in parallel with the domain ontology evolution.

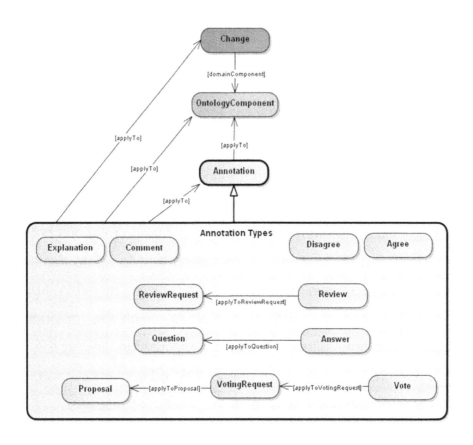

Figure 3.12 Annotation Subtypes with semantic relations.

Thus, an annotation can be classified into one of the types below, according to the context of the environment:

Explanation: optional comment inserted to justify any change in the ontology. It has the semantic relation *applyToChange* relating it to change. Corresponds to the element *Justification* of IBIS.

Comment: free comment inserted anytime. Has the semantic relation ApplyTo relating it to a change, an annotation or a component of the ontology.

Agree: comment used if you agree with some component of the ontology, change or annotation. Has the semantic relation ApplyTo, relating it to a change, an annotation or a component of the ontology.

Disagree: comment used if you disagree with any part of the ontology, change or annotation. Has semantic relation ApplyTo, relating it to a change, an annotation or a component of the ontology. Corresponds to the element *Challenge* of IBIS.

ReviewRequest: comment inserted when you want other users to review particular artifact. Has the semantic relation ApplyTo, relating it to a change, an annotation or a component of the ontology.

Review: comment inserted when reviewing particular artifact, after a request for review. Has the semantic relation applyToReviewRequest, relating it to an annotation of type ReviewRequest.

Question: comment inserted when asking something to other users. Has the semantic relation ApplyTo, relating it to a change, a note or a component of the ontology. Corresponds to the element *Issue* of IBIS.

Answer: comment inserted when answering certain subject, after some question. Has the semantic relation applyToQuestion, relating it to an annotation of type Question. Corresponds to the element *Idea* of IBIS.

Proposal: inserted comment when proposing something to other users. Has semantic relation ApplyTo, relating it to a change, a note or a component of the ontology.

VotingRequest: comment inserted when requiring users to vote on the change proposal. Has the semantic relation applyToProposal, relating it to an annotation of type Proposal.

Vote: comment inserted when voting on a particular topic, after some vote request. Has the semantic relation applyToVotingRequest, relating it to an annotation of type VotingRequest.

This proposed model directs the discussions, creating well structured communication flows and well-defined semantics, making the annotations a very important resource to complement the collaborative development of a domain ontology. The different annotation types, with different meanings, avoids unstructured discussions. Thus, the discussion is directed to the annotation types used, for example, if a user makes an annotation of type Question, other users can only generate annotations of type Answer, as well as when a user creates a VotingRequest, other users may only answer with Vote annotations types, related to the request annotation. The different types of annotation and possible subsequent annotations can be seen in Table 3.1.

Table 3.1 Annotation types and possible subsequent notes

Annotation	Subsequent Possible annotations
Question	Answer
Answer	Agree / Disagree / Question / Proposal
Review Request	Review / Question
Review	Agree / Disagree / Question / Proposal
Proposal	Vote Request / Agree / Disagree / Question
Vote Request	Vote / Question
Vote	Agree / Disagree / Question
Comment	Agree / Disagree / Question / Proposal
Agree	Agree / Disagree / Question / Proposal
Disagree	Agree / Disagree / Question / Proposal

We believe that the classification of annotations into different types causes every discussion process, in the ending, to generate changes in the domain ontology, reaching the ultimate goal of the collaboration.

3.3 Collaboration Environment Specification

In this section, collaborative environment is described in a structural way in order to define the components that are part of it and their relationships. The environment includes the types of users who access the system and constructs available in the metadata layer to represent the domain ontology and collaboration. Thus, we can formally define the collaboration environment as follows:

$$S = [R, C, D1 .. Dn, H1 .. Hn, U, P]$$

Assuming that:

- **R** represents the representation metaontology;
- **C** represents the collaboration metaontology;
- **D1 .. Dn** represents one or more domain ontologies;
- **H1 .. Hn** represents one or more collaboration histories, one for each domain ontology;
- **U** represents the set of user types allowed to access the system;
- **P** represents the set of change operations defined in the collaboration ontology C users of type U have permission to perform in the environment. Thus, P is the mapping U x C → P.

Assuming that changes can be made by different users, some changes can only be made by certain user profiles or types. For example, a user profile "Knowledge Engineer" can make a change that involves ontological foundation (MudancaDeMetaPropriedade), while a user profile "Specialist" can not. Next, the presented elements are detailed:

$$R = [\ R_1..R_n\ ]$$

$$C = [\ C_1..C_n\ ]$$

$$D = [\ I^R_1..I^R_n\ ]$$

$$H = [\ I^C_1..I^C_n\ ]$$

$$U = [\ U^{ENGINEER},\ U^{EXPERT},\ U^{VISITOR}\ ]$$

$$P = [$$

$U^{ENGINEER} \times C^{ConceptMetaPropertyChange} \rightarrow$ **true,**

$U^{ENGINEER} \times C^{ConceptMetaTypeChange} \rightarrow$ **true,**

$U^{EXPERT} \times C^{ConceptMetaPropertyChange} \rightarrow$ **false,**

$U^{EXPERT} \times C^{ConceptMetaTypeChange} \rightarrow$ **false,**

$U^{VISITOR} \times C^{ConceptMetaPropertyChange} \rightarrow$ **false,**

$U^{VISITOR} \times C^{ConceptMetaTypeChange} \rightarrow$ **false,**

$U^{EXPERT} \times C^{ConceptCreated} \rightarrow$ **true,**

$U^{VISITOR} \times C^{AnnotationCreated} \rightarrow$ **true,**

etc...

$$]$$

$R_1..R_n$ are the Representation Ontology **(R)** metaconcepts that define the possible components that can be created in the domain ontology (concept, property, relation, etc..). $C_1..C_n$ are the Collaboration Ontology **(O)** metaconcepts that define the possible change events that can be created in the collaborative environment. $I^R_1..I^R_n$ represents one or more components of the domain ontology **(D)** (which are actually instances of the representation ontology, so represented with I^R). The collaboration history **(H)** is the set of instances of the collaborative ontology, containing all collaboration events (changes and annotations) that occurred in the process, represented by $I^C_1..I^C_n$. The set of types of users contains the types: $U^{ENGINEER}$, Knowledge Engineer, U^{EXPERT}, Expert and $U^{VISITOR}$, Visitor. The set of permissions P relate the combination of collaborative operations and the types of users with the ability to perform each operation.

To represent the visual attributes of ontological concepts and properties described in section 1.3, we formalized these ontological components defined in the representation ontology as follows:

$$R^C = (T_1..T_n \, , \, P_o..P_1, \, F_0..F_n)$$
$$R^P = (T_1..T_n, \, V_0..V_n)$$
$$V = (N1..Nn \, , \, P_o..P_1)$$

Where R^C are the ontological concepts, defined by the set $T_1..T_n$ representing the name (linguistic terms) for concept in each language, $P_o..P_1$ representing at most one pictorial icon linked to the concept and $F_0..F_n$ representing zero or more pictorial instances photos to exemplify the concept, R^P are the ontological properties, defined by the set $T_1..T_n$ representing the name (linguistic terms) of the property in each language and the set $V_0..V_n$ representing the possible values the property can assume for a given instance. Each possible value V has a linguistic term $T_1..T_n$ and at most a pictorial icon $P_0..P_1$.

In the next chapter we describe in detail the implementation of the environment for collaborative construction of knowledge using the ontologies developed in this work.

4 SOFTWARE ENGINEERING

The proposed tool consisted of an online system, accessible over the Internet, focused on meeting the requirements cited in this work through providing a domain ontology to experts and knowledge engineers so that they can modify and comment over the shared knowledge model. The system is responsible for documenting everything that happens in the process of collaboration in a simple interface for high usability.

Below, we describe the architecture of the tool which is based on layers and designed to support the use of metadata.

4.1 Architecture

The application was developed on the model of three layers (MVC - Model View Controller) Interface Layer, Model Layer and Business Layer. We use a data access layer to abstract additional handling triplets and other low-level functions to manipulate the ontology. Below, we explain each component of the architecture in detail.

The User Interface layer is responsible for building and rendering the visual components with which the user will interact, such as buttons, lists and forms.

The Model layer includes classes that define the basic components of the system. In case, you define the components of the domain ontology, based on their structure. The URI attribute is the unique identifier of an ontology component and is present in all components of the representation, collaboration and domain ontologies.

The Business Layer includes classes that implement the business rules that are responsible for the functionality of the system. The "intelligence" of the system is in that layer. This layer uses the data models defined in the Model layer. Next, we describe the main classes that constitutes this layer:

Authenticator: Infrastructure class, responsible for tracking user authentication by username and password;

ActiveSession: Infrastructure class, responsible for the control of active user session, ie, the management of data used in a particular system access;

InterfaceControl : Responsible for the interaction between the interface layer with other classes of business layer. Most methods are called directly through the interface.

OntologyTreeView : Responsible for controlling loading and assembling the tree of concepts;

DomainOntologyControl : Responsible for managing the domain ontology, defining how the ontology will be loaded and manipulated during the collaboration period.

ChangeControl : Responsible for controlling the collaboration, including methods for creating, changing and removing components of the ontology.

The Data Access Layer is responsible for abstracting the database access or other storage artifacts such as OWL files. This layer consists of three main classes:

DBHelper: responsible for managing connections to the database.

OntologyManager: responsible for managing the triple format subject, predicate, object. This class is widely used by the class ChangeControl, from business layer.

OWLManager: responsible for reading or generating OWL files.

4.2 Data Persistence

Within the information systems context, an ontology is an engineering artifact that uses a specific vocabulary to describe a certain reality. We know that a domain ontology is a formal specification of a shared group knowledge on a particular area of interest [5]. However, a highly informal ontology is not an ontology because it can not be understood by a computer [33]. For this reason, an ontology must be represented by a formal language such as RDF or OWL. The Resource Description Framework (RDF) is a language which actually consists of a data model of metadata used to model conceptual descriptions of resources. The Web Ontology Language (OWL) is a language for knowledge representation based on RDF and characterized by allowing the expression of formal semantics and first order logic usage. Both are suitable for the storage of ontologies by W3C [4].

However, it is also possible to store metadata in RDF or OWL database using Triple Stores. The Triple Stores stores all the information only with a object-attribute-value triple, using one or more tables and retrieving information with SQL extended query languages, such as SPARQL (SPARQL Protocol and RDF Query Language) or directly via SQL (Structured Query Language).

4.3 Interaction with OWL Language

Looking for compatibility with current standards, it is possible to establish a correspondence between the main components of the representation ontology and OWL primitives, allowing the generation of a domain ontology in the system from existing ontologies in OWL or the generation of an OWL ontology from the system domain ontology.

When generating a domain ontology from an OWL ontology, the ontological components are imported in a generic way (for example, every class in OWL becomes one OntologyConcept the domain ontology) and then can be specialized in one of its subtypes (eg Sortal, Mixin, Role, etc..) during the stage of collaboration.

When generating the OWL ontology from the domain ontology, all semantic information already linked to ontological components through the system will be lost in this operation.

These two adaptations occur because OWL does not have precise enough primitive to store visual knowledge or ontological foundation, not allowing, for example, the specification of partonomic relations, metatypes concepts or pictorial components.

Table 4.1 shows the possible correspondence of the components of domain ontology with the OWL language primitives.

Table 4.1 Correspondence of the components of the representation ontology with OWL constructs.

Representation Ontology	Primitive OWL DL
Concept	*Class*
Relationship	*ObjectProperty*
Property	*DatatypeProperty*
Icon	*[No match]*
Photography	*[No match]*

5 VALIDATION

This chapter describes the validation approach for the proposed system and the planning of the assessment tool by end users, designed to identify the limitations of the proposed environment.

5.1 Domain Ontology Case Study

To validate the system in a real environment, we chose a study case in the domain of Sedimentary Stratigraphy, a Geology area specialized in the study of rock layers, which tries to determine the processes and events that formed them.

The Sedimentary Stratigraphy specifies the rocky bodies that form the Earth's crust and distinguish their units by identifying each rock type. To identify the portion of the rock, the expert often needs visual support to link the patterns of rock with some known category of rock. This justifies the use of visual components such as icons and photos when modeling domain knowledge in the form of ontology.

This domain was chosen primarily because it has some importance for our focus:

a) is strongly based on visual knowledge;

b) its structure is complex, involving many structural problems and disagreements among experts;

c) it has scientific and economic importance, because it studies the conditions of the current generation and spatial distribution of important mineral deposits such as coal and oil.

In Lorenzatti's work [26], a domain ontology was built with the help of experts in the domain of sedimentary stratigraphy, also seeking to associate icons with concepts and values of properties. This ontology served as the basis for initiating the collaboration stages of the system, ie the concepts, properties and relations were imported in collaboration system, providing an initial domain for the experts to judge the information, discuss and propose changes until a stable model of ontology is obtained, reflecting the shared domain conceptualization.

5.2 Evaluation

As a preliminary assessment of the environment, we provided the system to three users (two geologists and one knowledge engineer) for free usage for about six months, evolving a domain ontology previously built through interview processes with experts. Additionally, we proposed a validation system for the evaluation of collaborative tools.

5.2.1 Tool Usage by Test Users

The domain ontology built by Lorenzatti was available in OWL format, which allowed its importation into the collaborative system. This was done by converting OWL primitives into system ontology constructs, generating instances of the representation ontology metaconcepts. After, we invited a group of geology experts and students to analyze and propose new ontology changes, in order to consolidate it through the collaboration environment. The icons defined in Lorenzatti's work and new created icons were formally linked to the domain ontology by the experts during the collaboration process.

The test users used the system over three months, generating changes in concepts, properties and relations of the domain ontology. The quantitative scenario of the collaboration can be seen in Table 5.1.

After the analysis, we noticed that the number of concepts and properties increased after the collaboration due to the ontology expansion by users. The reduced number of relations is explained because the existing ontology had many properties incorrectly defined as relations for the difficulty of formalizing properties with default values (QualityStructure) in the tool which the ontology was first modeled. It may be noted that several changes were made in relation to the visual elements (icons) and foundational elements (metaproperties and metatypes), for the ability of the tool to work with these artifacts.

Table 5.1 Quantitative analysis of the collaboration performed on domain ontology.

ATTRIBUTE	BEFORE COLLABORATION	AFTER COLLABORATION
Number of Total Changes	Not Available	1485
Number of Total Concepts	121	183
Number of Total Properties	10	22
Number of Total Relations	28	15
Number of Total Icons	No	125
Number of Concepts Added	Not Available	93
Number of Concepts Deleted	Not Available	31
Number of Concepts Changed	Not Available	84
Number of Properties Added	Not Available	25
Number of Properties Excluded	Not Available	13
Number of additions Relations	Not Available	16
Number of Excluded Relations	Not Available	29

Number of icons linked to Concepts	No	26
Number of icons linked to Property Values	No	99
Number of Changes in metaproperties of Concepts	Not Available	63
Number of Metatypes changed manually by users	Not Available	5

5.2.2 Comparison Tool

To make a comparative analysis with existing tools for collaborative ontology based on the collaboration criteria defined in section 2.1.3, we built a comparative table of the current solutions our solution, as seen in Table 5.2.

Table 5.2 Table comparing the tools of collective construction of ontologies.

Criterion	Manufacturing	On-toEdit	NeOn Toolkit	Collaborative Protégé	We-bODE	Our Tool
Structured Discussion (Annotations)	NO	NO	YES	YES	NO	**YES**
Collaboration History	NO	NO	NO	YES	NO	**YES**
Support for OWL	NO	NO	YES	YES	YES	**YES**
Support for Inference	NO	YES	YES	YES	YES	**NO**
Inconsistencies Detection	NO	YES	YES	YES	YES	**NO**
Distinguished User Profiles	NO	NO	NO	NO	NO	**YES**
Intuitive Web Interface	YES	NO	NO	YES	NO	**YES**
Centralized Access via Web Browser	YES	YES	NO	YES	YES	**YES**

Allows use without for- mal ontology knowledge	YES	YES	YES	NO	NO	**YES**
Use in Visual Domains	NO	NO	NO	NO	NO	YES
Uses the methodology OntoClean	NO	YES	NO	NO	YES	YES
Uses Onto- logical Foun- dation	NO	NO	NO	NO	NO	YES

After comparison, we noticed that our tool meets its objectives by providing support for ontological foundation and visual domains, with an intuitive web interface. We know that the tool does not have automatic inference support, but constructed ontologies can be applied to any existing inference engine. Based on this, we assume that the tool fulfills its role in relation to its main objectives.

5.2.3 System Validation Method

To check for an impartial approach and the tool we built a validation method including indicators, metrics and issues. The validation tool can be used to assess both the proposed system when other similar approaches.

Initially, we define indicators for assessing the quality of the approach and the tool more precisely.

Below are the indicators of the intrinsic quality of the approach:

1. Support the choice for representation primitives
2. Modeling with more detail
3. Convergence of the collectively built model
4. Applicability of the built ontology

Below are the indicators of the intrinsic quality of the tool:

5. Easiness of modifying the existing ontology
6. Usability

To allow an effective measurement, specific evaluation metrics were defined for each indicator. Each of the metrics below is related to the same indicator number.

1. Number of constructs provided to represent the ontological objects.
2. Number of constructs in lower hierarchical levels to basic ontological constructs (concept, property, relation).
3. Time taken for the number of changes made in the ontology to be reduced to a certain limit (the limit may vary according to the number of users, size of the ontology, etc..).
4. Number of applications or projects mapped by the community of users that may directly or indirectly use the developed domain ontology.

5. Number of ontological objects changed in a given period, compared to the number of changed objects in a manual process of ontology development (assuming both ontologies are the same size).

6. Number of clicks required to access the most common features of ontology modification by users.

To measure these metrics, we developed questions to be answered by the group of users who use the collaborative tool, trying to get an initial idea and objective of the applicability and usefulness of the system in an impartial manner. Thus, we came up with the following questions:

1) **Regarding the association of domain concepts with appropriate representation primitives, it is possible to say that:** (This question is related to the metric 1)

   1 - The tool prevents the modeling task

   2 - The tool complicates the modeling task

   3 – Using the tool is equivalent of building ontologies manually

   4 - The tool helps the modeling task

   5 - The tool enables modeling that would not be possible to do manually

2) **The basic ontological components (concept, property, relation) have specialized constructs to represent them in proportion:** (This question is related to the metric 2)

   1 - Insufficient / You can only represent the basic components

   2 - Below Expected / Insufficient basic constructs to represent various components

   3 - Average / Some components do not have adequate constructs to represent them with expressiveness

   4 - Adequate / Some components do not have appropriate constructs, but without loss of representative expressiveness

   5 - Perfect / All components have adequate constructs to represent them with expressiveness

3) The elapsed time since the beginning of the collaboration until the ontology reached a common sense, enabling use it for other purposes was: (This question is related to the metric 3)

    1 - Exaggerated / Exceeded user expectation highly

    2 - High / Exceeded user expectation lightly

    3 - Adequate / It was within the expectations of the users

    4 - Reduced / It took less time than expected by users

    5 - Very Low / It took much less time than expected by users

4) How would you rate the ontology generated AFTER the collaboration process regarding its applicability in the real world, compared with the existing ontology BEFORE collaboration? (This question is related to the metric 4)

1 - Very Poor / The ontology could serve only as informal consultation

2 - Poor / The ontology could serve as input for systems or as informal consultation, but with the possibility to generate several errors

3 - Adequate / The ontology could serve as input for systems or as informal consultation, but with the possibility to generate fewer errors

4 - Good / The ontology could serve as input for some systems or for formal consultation

5 - Very Good / The ontology could serve as input for various systems or for formal consultation

5) **The number of ontological objects changed since the beginning of the collaboration until the ontology reached a common sense, compared to the number of ontological objects changde in the construction of the ontology using the manual process was:** (This question is related to the metric 5)

1 - Very Low / The manual process generated much more object changes than in the collaborative process

2 - Reduced / The manual process has generated changes in more objects than in the collaborative process

3 - Equivalent / The manual process changed about the same number of objects that the collaborative process

4 - High / The collaborative process led to changes in more objects than the manual process

5 - Very High / The collaborative process generated much more object changes than the manual process

6) **How would you rate the user interface of the tool regarding the ease of use (easy to access the desired features, clear interface, user interaction with the interface)?** (This question is related to the metric 6)

 1 - Very Bad / Can not use some features

 2 - Bad / Hard to use some features

 3 - Proper / Basic Functionality accessed easily but little clear and objective

 4 - Good / All features easily accessed though unclear

 5 - Very Good / All features are clear, easily accessible and objective

7) **How would you rate the user interface of the tool relative to other ontology editing tools you have used?** (This question is related to the metric 6)

 1 - Much worse / The other tools are extremely easier to use

 2 - Worst / Some tools are easier to use

 3 - Equivalent / The other tools have similar interface or with the same level of difficulty interaction

 4 - Best / Other tools are more difficult to operate than the system proposed

 5 - Very Best / The proposed system facilitates the editing of the ontology compared to other interface tools

Some indicators require an extended period of use of the tool so that they can be measured, ie, its applicability is only possible in the medium and long term, after several collaborative interactions of users in the system. Therefore, as the validation period of the tool was relatively small compared to the construction time of the approach and the tool, the metrics of indicators 3 and 4 could be measured effectively. On the other hand, the indicator 6 requires a comparation to a manual ontology development (data unavailable at the time of validation of this work). Because of these obstacles, we believe that the proposed validation system is very useful for future work.

With the answers to the questions, it is possible to construct a comparative table. The alternatives of the issues are related to a weight which together leads to a total value. The higher the value, the better the performance of the analysed tool, compared to the manual process. The weights are equal to the numbers of alternatives. For example, the alternative one (1) has the weight 1 (one) and benefits the manual process while the alternative five (5) has the weight 5 (five) and benefits the system automated collaborative process. Thus, to carry out validation, we suggest using Table 5.3, here with hypothetical data, shown below:

Table 5.3 Results of the evaluation questions of the tool (hypothetical data).

Points	1 User	User 2	User 3	Total
Question 1	1	2	3	6
Question 2	2	5	5	12
Question 3	3	2	2	7
Question 4	4	3	3	10
Question 5	5	4	1	10
Question 6	3	1	2	6
Question 7	1	3	5	9

In this example, the sum total of points for questions is 60. The total minimum would be 21 (assuming that the first three users responded to all questions), while the total maximum would be 105 (assuming that the three users answered to all five questions). The closer the total number is with 105, the greater the benefit of using the collaboration tool. We also suggest the creation of a threshold within this range (eg 80) to facilitate the identification when the tool reaches the minimum criteria to be accepted as valuable, so it meets the quality requirements of collaborative construction of ontologies.

As a comparative experiment, we also suggest comparing the construction of an ontology in the manual process, the analysed tool and three other current collaborative tools (eg Collaborative Protégé, and WebODE OntoEdit). In this process, would be defined fifteen (15) members, divided into groups of three (3) members for each approach / tool. Each group would be responsible for modeling an ontology formalizing the same conceptual problem presented to all groups (eg, model the operation in a bookstore), featuring the same period of time for the task. After modeling, the groups would be subject to assessment questions, for mounting the comparative table 5.4:

Table 5.4 Sum of points of evaluation questions of the tool, comparing different approaches (hypothetical data).

Points	Manual Procedure	Our Tool	Collaborative Protégé	WebODE	OntoEdit
Total Points	80	80	80	80	80

In addition, a comparative table may be constructed to measure , the ontological objects quantitatively, on each approach. This comparison can be seen in Table 6.5:

Table 5.5 Quantitative result of ontological objects and changes, comparing different approaches / tools for building ontology (hypothetical data).

Points	Manual Procedure	Our Tool	Collaborative Protégé	WebODE	OntoEdit
Number of Total Changes Outgo	1	1	1	1	1
Number of Total Concepts	1	1	1	1	1
Number of Total Properties	1	1	1	1	1
Number of Total Relations	1	1	1	1	1
Number of Total Icons	1	1	1	1	1
Number of Concepts Added	1	1	1	1	1
Number of Concepts Deleted	1	1	1	1	1
Number of Concepts Changed	1	1	1	1	1
Number of Properties Added	1	1	1	1	1
Number of Proper-	1	1	1	1	1

ties Excluded					
Number of additions Relations	1	1	1	1	1
Number of Exclud-ed Relations	1	1	1	1	1
Number of icons linked to concepts	1	1	1	1	1
Number of icons linked to Property Values	1	1	1	1	1
Number of Changes in metaproperties of Concepts	1	1	1	1	1
Number of Metatypes sorted manually by users	1	1	1	1	1

After these assessments it will be possible to identify more clearly the benefits of the analysed tool in comparison with other similar proposals.

In the following chapter, we present the conclusions of this work and anticipate some future work, as an expansion of the goals already achieved.

6 CONCLUSION

Ontologies are conceptual models derived from explicit knowledge shared by a group of users focused on a specific area of interest. The main goal of ontologies is to facilitate the communication of knowledge between individuals of a community through explicit semantic relations between concepts of reality, ie, establish consensual knowledge in a generic and formal way [6].

Because it is an shared artifact and is focused on consensus, an ontology is built only after several interactions between participants contemplating different views and levels of experts' knowledge. In some cases, an ontology can take years to achieve a cohesive enough state to be used as formal consultation or to support computer systems. This long time is due to the difficulty of finding consensus in a community, because the more knowledge and restrictions are imposed on the model by users, the greater the need for effective communication between them. Communication allows the transfer of experience between humans and the collective construction of solutions increasing the capacity field of environment.

Moreover, as we saw earlier, the information domains are not static: they evolve when missing elements become part of the domain or when some elements become obsolete [30]. Thus, the conceptual problem of classifying the world entities becomes even more complicated because each individual has its own abstraction of reality (which can be in constant update). This difficulty is even harder when several people discuss over the same shared conceptual model, when divergent ideas and conceptualizations can arise.

The support by a software tool makes the process of ontology building more efficient and productive, facilitating communication between users and the storage of the knowledge involved in the process. We believe that, with the advent of Web 2.0, collaboration becomes a trend and that the union of the aspects of mass cooperation with semantic formalization of ontologies becomes an important step to be taken in the area of Knowledge Engineering. Thus, in this work we proposed the construction of a collaborative system for creating ontologies on the web.

According to [17], the conversational maximum for building conceptual models is that the message should be relevant full, clear, unambiguous, brief, without information excess and real through the point of view of the sender's knowledge. Thus, just the creation of a knowledge model is not enough, it also must be semantically valid so it can be efficiently used. This is done by comparing the level of homomorphism between a concrete object of reality and its representation in a formal and explicit conceptualization, through the analysis of the properties that classify isomorphism of conceptual models: Clarity, Correctness, Completeness and Laconicity.

We have seen that problems arise when we create diagrams with lack of these properties: a) non-lucid diagrams occur when there is an overload in the specification constructs, ie when more than one concept of the model map to the same construct generating ambiguity b) non-correct diagrams occur when specification constructs do not map to the conceptualization entities, generating an excess of constructs c) non-laconic diagrams occur when model concepts are mapped to more than one construct the specification, generating constructs redundancy and unnecessary complexity to represent d) incomplete diagrams occur when some model concepts cannot be mapped to constructs, creating a lack of specification expressiveness to represent certain conceptualization entities.

To guide the creation of more cohesive diagrams, we note that the use of a foundational ontology plays an important role in achieving the common consensus, reducing the possibilities of interpretation over the domain through the semantic categorization of concepts and properties of the ontology. A foundational ontology aims to establish a base to obtain consistency in the meaning negotiations arised from the collaboration of individuals on a conceptual model. Guizzardi [16] proposed a unified foundational ontology which provides an ontological foundation to build conceptual models. The constructs proposed by Guizzardi guide the construction of the knowledge model, assisting in taxonomic classification and relationships establishment between concepts. Thus, the occurrence of ambiguities decreases and the accuracy of the domain model increases.

We discussed the state of the art of ontology editors and introduced aspects of collaboration that guide the development of collaboration systems. In fact, the current collaborative ontology editors have several important features such inconsistency detection, inference, documentation, validation, consultation, integration, etc.. However, many of them can not be accessed via a web browser, which can be a serious problem these days. None of the current approaches make use of a foundational ontology. Also, some applications are strongly oriented to the representation language or ontological formalism. In such cases, the tools do not abstract technical information for the specialist or do not provide an intuitive enough interface to prevent the user be afraid to change the ontology freely. This often creates barriers in the collaborative construction of ontologies, affecting the creation of correct models.

In our proposal, we implemented a collaborative web system, accessible via web browser, which allows experts to directly change the ontology, recording all changes automatically. We used a base metadata layer to provide foundational ontological constructs to support the ontological choices through the semantic expressiveness of a foundational ontology, along with collaborative artifacts to allow a mapping of ontological changes and discussions held between community members.

A model for structured discussion was also proposed, based on consolidated solutions as DILIGENT and IBIS, formalizing the use of annotations linked to ontology elements or change events. The mapping of the discussions enables to access detailed conversation history to track changes in the domain ontology or detect the precise moments when ontological decisions are made. This is an improvement compared to existing editors as it introduces a wider range of types of interactions in the discussion and restrict its use in relation to the previous interaction, linking the arguments according to its semantics.

In our proposal, the tool has features that allow users or community experts to define concepts, properties and relations, making explicit their intended meaning through the use of foundational ontology primitives. However, the construction of ontologies is a task that requires knowledge about conceptual modeling, which brings difficulty for domain experts to build well founded ontologies themselves. Thus, in our proposal, it is possible to formally introduce the role of the knowledge engineer as an user acting in collaboration, focused on monitoring, fixing and choosing the best symbolic anchoring between the modeled concepts and the representation primitives.

There are information areas where visual knowledge is crucial for its completeness. In these imagistic areas, visual pattern recognition is the initial process to capture information and support problem solving. We could not found an application for building ontologies that uses imagistic components. The use of visual primitives such as images and icons allows for a greater understanding of the domain where the symbolic linguistic representation is not sufficient to explain certain knowledge. One of the goals of the proposed tool was to provide ontological constructs for representing visual knowledge and support imagistic domains in collaborative construction of domain ontologies.

This study focused on the phenomenon of collective collaboration as a tool to support the construction of ontologies, taking into account the importance of ontological foundation and visual knowledge. To support and formalize interactions in an collaborative environment, we used a conceptual basis for modeling the 3C collaboration model [9]. This model argues that, to collaborate, individuals must exchange information (communicate), organize (coordinate) and operate together in a shared space (cooperate). These concepts formed the conceptual basis for the implementation of specific functionalities in the system and for the collaborative approach as a whole.

Finally, the developed tool has important differences compared to existing tools, mainly because it provides an collaborative environment for the web, focused on constructing explicit shared knowledge models, or domain ontologies, by using accurate and expressive representation constructs, derived from ontological foundation concepts and visual components. Thus, we can say that this work has contributed to a conceptual approach and innovative tool, focused on allowing the construction of ontologies even more rich and applicable to commercial use.

LIST OF ABBREVIATIONS AND ACRONYMS

IBIS	*Issue-based Information System*
IEEE	*Institute of Electrical and Electronics Engineers*
MVC	*Model View Controller*
OWL	*Ontology Web Language*
RDF	*Resource Description Framework*
SPARQL	*Protocol and RDF Query Language*
SQL	*Structured Query Language*
UFO	*Unified Foundational Ontology*
W3C	*World Wide Web Consortium*

REFERENCES

[1] ABEL, M. Estudo da perícia em petrografia sedimentar e sua importância para a engenharia de conhecimento. 2002. 239 f. Tese de Doutorado (Programa de Pós-Graduação em Computação) - Instituto de Informática - Universidade Federal do Rio Grande do Sul, Porto Alegre.

[2] ADAMCZYK, P.D.; TWIDALE, M.B. Supporting multidisciplinary collaboration: requirements from novel HCI education. Proceedings of the SIGCHI conference on Human factors in computing systems, ACM, New York, USA, p. 1073–1076, 2007.

[3] ARPÍREZ, J.C. et al. WebODE: a scalable workbench for ontological engineering. Proceedings of the 1st international conference on Knowledge capture., ACM, K-CAP '01, New York, USA, p. 6–13, 2001.

[4] BERNERS-LEE, T. et al. The semantic web. Scientific American, vol. 279, Number 5, p. 35-43, 2001 [S.l.].

[5] BORST, W.N. Construction of Engineering Ontologies for Knowledge Sharing and Reuse. Ph.D. Dissertation, Centre for Telematics and Information Technology, University of Twente, Enschede, The Netherlands, 1997.

[6] CORCHO, O.; FERNANDEZ-LOPEZ, M.; GÓMEZ-PÉREZ, A. Methodologies, tools and languages for building ontologies. Where

is their meeting point?. Data & Knowledge Engineering, 46(1), p.41–64, 2003 [S.l.].

[7] DELLSCHAFT, K. et al. Tracking design rationale in collaborative ontology engineering. The Semantic Web: Research and Applications, Springer. Berlin Heidelberg, 2008. p.782–786.

[8] FERNANDEZ-LOPEZ, M.; GÓMEZ-PÉREZ, A.; JURISTO, N. Methontology: from ontological art towards ontological engineering. Proceedings of the AAAI97 Spring Symposium Series on Ontological Engineering, Stanford, USA, 1997, p. 33–40.

[9] FUKS, H., GEROSA, M., PIMENTEL, M. Projeto de Comunicação em Groupware: Desenvolvimento, Interface e Utilização. XXII Jornada de Atualização em Informática, Anais do XXIII Congresso da Sociedade Brasileira de Computação, 2003. p. 295–338.

[10] GÓMEZ-PÉREZ, A.; FERNANDEZ-LOPEZ, M.; CORCHO, O. Ontological Engineering: with examples from the areas of Knowledge Management, e-Commerce and the Semantic Web. 1rd ed. (Advanced Information and Knowledge Processing), Springer-Verlag New York, Inc, 2004. 420 p.

[11] GRUBER, T.R. Toward principles for the design of ontologies used for knowledge sharing. International Journal of Human Computer Studies, 43(5) , 1995, p.907–928 [S.I.].

[12] GUARINO, N. Concepts, attributes and arbitrary relations: Some linguistic and ontological criteria for structuring knowledge bases. Data & Knowledge Engineering, 8(3) , 1992, p.249–261 [S.I.].

[13] GUARINO, N., Formal Ontology in Information Systems. Proceedings of FOIS'98, Trento, Italy, 1998, p. 6-8.

[14] GUARINO, N. Formal ontology, conceptual analysis and knowledge representation. International Journal of Human Computer Studies, 43(5), 1995, p.625–640 [S.I.].

[15] GUIZZARDI G. et al. Ontologias de Fundamentação e Modelagem Conceitual, II Seminário de Pesquisa em Ontologia no Brasil, IME, Rio de Janeiro, 2009.

[16] GUIZZARDI, G. et al. An Ontologically Well-Founded Profile for UML Conceptual Models. A. Persson, J. Stirna (eds.) Advanced Information Systems Engineering, Proceedings of 16th CAiSE Conference, Riga, Springer, 2004. p. 1–122.

[17] GUIZZARDI, G. Ontological Foundations for Structural Conceptual Models. Enschede, The Netherlands: Universal Press, v.05-74. 2005. 410 p. (CTIT PhD Thesis Series), 2005.

[18] GUIZZARDI, G.; WAGNER, G. A unified foundational ontology and some applications of it in business modeling. Workshop on Enterprise Modeling and Ontologies for Interoperability, 16th Interna-

tional Conference on Advanced Information Systems Engineering (CAISE), Riga, 2004. p 129-143.

[19] HAASE, P. et al. The Neon Ontology Engineering Toolkit. WWW 2008 Developers Track, 2008 [S.I.].

[20] HARTMANN, J. et al. DEMO - Design Environment for Metadata Ontologies. Proceedings of the 3rd European Semantic Web Conference, ESWC 2006. Volume 4011. Budva, Montenegro. Springer Berlin, 2006. p.427–441.

[21] HENKE, J. Towards a Usable Group Editor for Ontologies. *The Semantic Web-ISWC 2006*, 2006, p.978–979 [S.I.].

[22] INSTITUTE OF ELECTRICAL AND ELECTRONIC ENGINEERING. IEEE Std 1074-1995: IEEE Standard for Developing Software Life Cycle Processes. IEEE Computer Society. New York, 1996.

[23] JOHN, M.; MELSTER, R. Knowledge networks–managing collaborative knowledge spaces. Advances in Learning Software Organizations, 6th International Workshop, LSO 2004, Banff, Canada, Springer, 2004. p.165–171.

[24] KUNZ, W.; RITTEL, H.W.J. Issues as Elements of Information Systems. Working Paper Number 131, Studiengruppe für Systemforschung, Heidelberg, Germany, July 1970.

[25] LORENZATTI, A. Ontologia para Domínios Imagísticos: Combinando Primitivas Textuais e Pictóricas. 2009. 117 f. Dissertação de

Mestrado, Universidade Federal do Rio Grande do Sul, Porto Alegre.

[26] LORENZATTI, A. et al. Ontological Primitives for Visual Knowledge. Advances in Artificial Intelligence SBIA 2010. São Bernardo do Campo: Springer, v.6404, 2011. p.1–10.

[27] MANGIONE, G.R. et al. A Pedagogical Approach for Collaborative Ontologies Building. Technology-Enhanced Systems and Tools for Collaborative Learning Scaffolding, 350/2011, 2011. p. 135-166.

[28] NOY, N.F.; TUDORACHE, T. Collaborative ontology development on the (semantic) web. AAAI Spring Symposium on Semantic Web and Knowledge Engineering (SWKE), Stanford, CA, 2008.

[29] OLIVEIRA, L. et al. Collective construction of Information Science through a Web 2.0 environment. International Workshop on Metamodels, Ontologies and Semantic Technologies, ONTOBRAS-MOST 2011, Gramado, Rio Grande do Sul, 2011.

[30] PALMA DE LEON, R. A. Ontology metadata management in distributed environment. Doctoral thesis. Universidad Politécnica de Madrid, Madrid, Spain, 2009.

[31] PRESS, N. Understanding Metadata. NISO Press Booklets, US, ISBN, 1-880124–62-9, 2004 [S.l.].

[32] RICHARDS, D. A social software/Web 2.0 approach to collaborative knowledge engineering. Information Sciences, 179(15) , 2009. p.2515–2523.

[33] STUDER, R.; BENJAMINS, V.R.; FENSEL, D. Knowledge engineering: principles and methods. Data & knowledge engineering, 25(1-2), 1998, p.161–197.

[34] SURE, Y. et al. OntoEdit: Collaborative ontology development for the semantic web. The Semantic Web—ISWC 2002, 2002, p.221–235.

[35] TUDORACHE, T. et al. Supporting collaborative ontology development in Protégé. The Semantic Web-ISWC 2008, 2008, p.17–32.

[36] USCHOLD, M.; GRUNINGER, M. Ontologies: Principles, methods and applications. The Knowledge Engineering Review, 11(02) , 1996, p.93–136.

www.ingramcontent.com/pod-product-compliance
Lightning Source LLC
LaVergne TN
LVHW041214050326
832903LV00021B/620